THE WHITE-WATER RIVER BOOK

THE WHITE-WATER RIVER BOOK

A Guide to Techniques, Equipment, Camping, and Safety

Pacific Search Press

by Ron Watters   Photographs by Robert Winslow

Pacific Search Press, 222 Dexter Avenue North,
    Seattle, Washington 98109
© 1982 by Ron Watters. All rights reserved
Printed in the United States of America

Edited by Betsy Rupp Fulwiler
Designed by Judy Petry
Illustrated by Ron Lewis

Photographs are by Robert Winslow except those by the following:
    Seth Ellis—page 140
    Robert Harrison—pages 19, 147, 148
    "H" Hilbert—pages 36, 153
    Nicki Holmes—page v (Dedication)
    Rob Lesser—pages 30–31, 101, 120
    Skip Peterson—pages 26, 98, 151

Library of Congress Cataloging in Publication Data

Watters, Ron.
    The White-Water River Book.

    Bibliography: p.
    Includes index.
    1. Rafting (Sports)   2. White-water canoeing.
3. Camping.   I. Title.
GV780.W37   797.1′22   82-2164
ISBN 0-914718-66-5   AACR2

Wherever you go and whatever you do in the outdoors, move at Nature's pace, seeking not to impose yourself but to lose yourself. If you must leave footprints, make them not with blindness but with care and awareness of the delicate balance around you. And if you must take souvenirs, take them not in your pockets but in your mind and spirit. In preservation lies the promise of renewal.

Pacific Search Press

This book is dedicated to a short, hairy, flamboyant man, who when I met him looked much like a Saturday night TV wrestler, with a black bikini swimsuit, black wet-suit bootees, and black tennis shoes. He was distinguishable above the noise of the river's rapids by his lusty laugh; by his ever-present Mae West life jacket; and by the kind of white water he ran—some of the biggest, most difficult white water anyone had ever run, breaking the barriers of white-water river running. He was a well-publicized symbol, revered and copied by some, criticized by others. But there is no doubt that this sincere and warm man ushered in a new age of explosive growth in kayaking and white-water river running.

To the fond memory of that special man, Walt Blackadar, this book is dedicated.

CONTENTS

PREFACE

As you might gather from the title, this is a book about how to run white-water rivers enjoyably and safely by kayak, oar raft, or paddle raft. How this actually is accomplished, however, varies greatly from region to region and from person to person. During the research for this book, I repeatedly found myself consulting with two highly respected boaters, both advocating completely opposing views on a topic. Yet each of their views was valid, working well for them and the rivers they run.

What I have tried to do in many portions of the text is to incorporate other views rather than present one side or my own opinions. This, I hope, will give you options from which you can select equipment and techniques that work for you. At the same time, I have tried to keep the text to a manageable length, substituting illustrative material in the place of wordy explanations.

This book covers a wide range of information about river running, but perhaps I should say a few words about what it does not cover. It is not about mechanized river travel. Everything discussed within, except the driving to and from the river, is done by paddle or oar power. White-water river running involves floating with the current, sometimes swiftly down a rapid, sometimes slowly and peacefully down quieter portions. Introducing motors in the river environment is incongruous, foreign, and obscene. Let motors be used on reservoirs—the dead, decaying portions of once healthy, free-flowing rivers. The political stratagems undertaken by a few Colorado River guides that successfully thwarted the National Park Service's well-researched plans to phase out motors on the Grand Canyon of the Colorado is one of the most dismal chapters of river management and a sad loss to those who seek a pristine, serene experience. There must be refuges where a person can come close to his surroundings and travel at a pace dictated by nature. Free-flowing white-water rivers should be such places.

This book also is not for the person who wants to sit back while a guide rows him down the river. It is for active people who want to learn how to run boats, organize trips, read white water, and camp along the banks of a river. It is for people who are willing to assume personal responsibility for their own safety by preparing adequately and striving to be as self-sufficient as possible while on the river. It is for people who are willing to put out the extra effort to reap a greater reward.

Let's hear it for free-flowing wild rivers—and all the personal challenges, the self-realizations, and the wonders and the joys they have to offer. May they always flow free.

Salmon River
River of No Return Wilderness

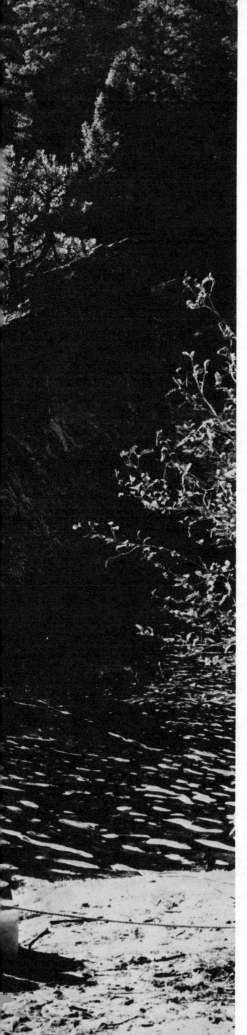

Few books about outdoor topics are the work of one person, and this book is no exception. No individual possibly can learn all there is to know or keep abreast of developments occurring in a sport that is growing and evolving as rapidly as white-water river running is. I have been fortunate to enlist the generous help of many authorities, manufacturers, and boaters in the mainstream of the sport who have taken the time to provide valuable input. My sincere thanks go to the following individuals: Charlie Walbridge, Wildwater Designs, Penllyn, Pennsylvania; O. K. Goodwin, Safety Chairman, American Whitewater Affiliation, Big Bar, California; Tom Wilson, Phoenix Products, Tyner, Kentucky; B. A. Hanten, Rogue Inflatables, Grants Pass, Oregon; Payson Kennedy, Les Bechdel, and Bunny Johns, all of the Nantahala Outdoor Center, Bryson City, North Carolina; Reg Lake, River Touring Equipment, Brisbane, California; Dick Held, Whitewater Boats, Cedar City, Utah; Richard Ford, Maravia Corporation, San Leandro, California; Jeff Bevan, Salmon River Boatworks, Salmon, Idaho; Pete Skinner, President, American Whitewater Affiliation, West Sand Lake, New York, New York; Ron Mattson, Cascade Outfitters, Monroe, Oregon; Steve Carothers, Museum of Northern Arizona, Flagstaff, Arizona; Bob Blackadar, Salmon, Idaho; Eric Leaper, Executive Director, National Organization for River Sports, Colorado Springs, Colorado; Pat Agidius, Northwest River Supplies, Moscow, Idaho; Mike Snead, Sierra Kayak School, Lotus, California; Ken Horwitz, Perception, Liberty, South Carolina; and Sue Villard, Rob Lesser, "H" Hilbert, and Tom Whittaker, all of Idaho.

I cannot thank these people enough for helping to make this book as accurate and current as possible. But I should make it clear that any errors, inaccuracies, and opinions expressed within are solely mine and in no way are those of people who have provided assistance.

The photographic work for the book was a time-consuming, difficult project, but it was made easier by the many patient boating companions who waited while cameras were set up and photos were taken again and again. My special thanks to all those who put up with Bob Winslow and me during those long days. Debbie Hatch-Winslow deserves recognition for her welcome assistance during the photographic sessions.

The illustrative material would not have been complete without the fine material available from white-water photographers in different areas. My thanks to the following photographers, who provided a pool of hundreds of additional photographs from which we could make selections: Robert Harrison, Seth Ellis, Dick Held, Rob Lesser, "H" Hilbert, Howard Moyer, Sue Villard, Skip Peterson, Ken Adraska, Errol Green, Jim Fullerton, and John Viehman of *Canoe* magazine.

Thanks to Bill Edwards of Wellington Mills for the data on rope characteristics; to Kathy Daly and Patti Dove for their editing assistance; to Carrol Hudson for typing; to Bob for his fine photographic work. And to the many wonderful friends throughout the years who have shared with me the good and bad days, the evenings around the campfires, and the peace of the river go my heartfelt thanks.

GETTING STARTED

Several years ago I planned a two-week-long trip on a river system in central Idaho. A woman in her sixties who ran a day-care center in California heard about the trip from a friend and wrote me a letter inquiring about it. I scribbled off a quick reply and told her we would love to have her join us.

She was enthusiastic about going on the trip, but from my quickly written letter, she did not really understand the nature of it. When she arrived in Idaho, she expected to find the trip run by a professional river guide who would take care of all the plans and arrangements.

What she found instead was a loosely organized group of people, many of whom did not know much more than she did about running rivers. Far from a guided trip, our party was a group of friends and acquaintances. Everyone was helping to plan the trip, buy food, pack gear, run boats, and do all the many other things necessary to get a group trip down a river. Some of the people had quite a bit of experience running white water. The plan was for these people to teach the basics to those with little or no experience.

The casual arrangement surprised the woman. She was by far the oldest member of the group and, as she looked at the young, mostly inexperienced members, she was not sure she wanted to go along. But she had not come all the way for nothing and decided to give it a try. Later she confided in me that, after looking our group over the first evening, she did not give herself much chance of making it back to California alive.

She was the kind of woman who does not like sitting around and quickly jumped in, helping with the cooking, cleaning, loading of boats, and other chores. She even helped row boats in the quieter stretches. After the tension of the first few days had worn off, she began to enjoy herself. Even though she ran the boats only in easy water, she contributed as much to the group as anybody else. She quickly became a hit with the college-aged members of the party, who enjoyed her quick smile and motherly words of wisdom before dropping into a rapid.

When the trip was over and everyone was leaving, we found it difficult to say good-bye to the woman who had been so special to have along with us.

Months later, she wrote me a letter and said that the trip was a highlight of her life and that she would always cherish the memories of those days on the river.

Whether river trips take an afternoon, a day, or many days, their intrinsic worth is illustrated by the California woman's experience. River

Good times, good folks

trips are a combination of many things: the excitement of white water, the warmth of an evening fire, the special thrills of watching wildlife, and the companionship and friendship that develop in groups when these experiences have been shared together.

Few activities offer the exhilaration felt when riding a boat into the splashing waves and frothing foam of rapids, intimately facing nature in one of its rawest displays of power and beauty. Yet most white-water rivers also provide a contrast to their untamed, turbulent parts. Between rapids, peaceful stretches of placid current allow a river runner to pause and to relax, slowing down his pace to match the rhythm of the quiet surroundings.

Of all the activities in the outdoors, a river trip is one that many different types of people can enjoy—young, old, rich, poor, physically fit, physically not-so-fit. All that is necessary is curiosity, a desire for some adventure, a willingness to learn some basic skills, and a love and respect for the outdoors.

Perhaps the most worthwhile attraction of river trips is that they provide a means by which people who normally are unable to can visit wilderness and patches of wild country. A good friend of mine was involved in a tragic accident, severing his right foot, around Thanksgiving time. The loss was particularly hard on him as he was an active hiker, sailor, and climber, his climbing travels having taken him to many places in the world. After a series of operations that winter, he recovered enough to start kayaking a little. He perfected a method of bracing himself in a kayak and began tackling day stretches on rivers. In a short time, he was off on a week-long trip down a wilderness river. Upon returning, he looked healthier and brighter, and said to me, "That's the best therapy I could have ever had."

Tom, of course, is not the only handicapped person to learn how to kayak or to run a boat. Blind people have learned to kayak and run rivers. And more and more, white-water schools and groups are offering special instructional sessions for handicapped boaters.

I have attended various congressional hearings to testify on behalf of conservationists' efforts to protect wilderness areas and wild rivers. At these hearings, some people invariably accuse conservationists of trying to protect a resource that only the young and extraordinarily fit can enjoy. However, a growing number of handicapped and blind people and senior citizens know differently.

Where

In order to have white water, a river must drop from a higher elevation to a lower elevation. Because of this, states, provinces, or countries where the terrain is relatively flat have little or no white water. The wheat fields of Kansas or the prairies of southern Saskatchewan, for example, are not good places to look for white-water rivers. On the other hand, if a river tumbles downward, losing elevation, white water will be found. Mountainous areas are obviously the best places to find it.

The choice of white-water rivers is broad. In the United States, dozens of white-water guidebooks describe hundreds of rivers to run. Rivers range from the well-known Grand Canyon of the Colorado to the wild Chattooga on the Georgia–South Carolina line.

Despite massive dams and irrigation projects in California, river runners still clash with the rousing rapids of the scenic Merced and Tuolumne rivers, plunging out of the Yosemite National Park area. To the north, flowing through an impressive granite gorge, is the lively South Fork of the American River. Farther still to the north, in "Big Foot" country, is the Klamath, with its splendid boating and fishing.

The Pacific Northwest of the United States is famous for such rivers as the Rogue, Zane Grey's favorite locale for his western stories, and many not-so-famous but equally challenging crystal blue coastal rivers that drop through opulent greenery to the ocean.

Unforgettable, multi-day journeys can be taken on the outstanding rivers of the Rocky Mountain region, with the Salmon River, Hells Canyon of the Snake, Yampa, Green, and others attracting crowds of boaters.

Equally impressive are the rivers found in another mecca of white-water boating, the southeastern United States. Here boaters do not have the long river journeys that western boaters have, but the rapids are as challenging and exciting as any found elsewhere. The extensive list includes the Youghiogheny of Pennsylvania, the Dead River and the West Branch of the Penobscot of Maine, the Wolf of Wisconsin, and so on.

I have touched on only a small minority of the rivers in the United States. Plenty more await exploration. Although many boaters flock to the popular rivers, it makes good environmental sense to seek out the lesser-known rivers. This not only helps spread the use of rivers and takes some pressure off heavily used areas, but it also allows boaters to get away from crowds.

Canada is blessed with an abundance of rivers, which Canadians have long appreciated. According to some estimates, as high as fourteen percent of all Canadians over the age of eighteen canoe. Much of Canada's white water has been run by this traditional mode of transportation, but many people also are using kayaks and inflatable rafts. In British Columbia, rafting is becoming so popular that visitor days on commercial trips alone are expected to double at least three times during the eighties. White water in British Columbia is found on such strong and swift rivers as the Thompson, the Fraser, and the Chilcotin. Neighboring Alberta boasts good white-water streams churning out of the magnificent Rockies.

White water stretches across Canada to Ontario, where kayaking is popular on such rivers as the Madawaska and the big rapids of the Ottawa. Farther east, more great wild rivers are found in Newfoundland and Labrador.

In Europe most of the larger rivers have been developed, leaving only smaller streams for boating. Popular white-water rivers are found in Germany, France, Austria, Spain, Switzerland, and Yugoslavia. The southern French Alps are preferred by many kayakers on the continent because the weather is almost always warm and dry in summer, the wine is good, and a range of different rivers is available for kayakers of all abilities. The Guil is a particularly impressive French river rushing through a narrow gorge just wide enough for a kayak. A centuries-old castle, Château-Queyras, is perched high above the sheer walls of the gorge.

To the north, Norway and Sweden are laced with exquisite white-water rivers. The Sjoa River in Norway is an invigorating, beautiful river that is runnable late into summer.

Across the ocean to South America, to the adventurous kayaking rivers of New Zealand, to Africa, and on to the great rivers of the Himalayas, white water abounds. Whether it is close to your home or a ways away, the rivers are out there waiting for the blade of your paddle or oar to break their surfaces.

Guil River in French Alps. Its dramatic canyon is so narrow that in many places it is impossible to turn a kayak sideways.

Getting Experience

White water has a way of quickly sorting out people who are inexperienced. Attempting a river that is harder than you are ready for may result in a bad experience: a chilly swim, overturned boat, wet gear, and maybe injury.

A boating friend of mine can attest to the value of starting gradually. Twelve years ago in Colorado, he and several other friends built kayaks in his garage. They did not know much about kayaking, but that did not deter them. Excitement ran high, and they could not wait to challenge the wetness and wildness of a river. Purchasing fiber glass cloth and resin, they formed the boats on a mold. The boats that eventually popped out were monstrous, heavy things, but were adequate for use on rivers.

For their first run in the new boats they chose sections I through VI of the Arkansas River in high water, a particularly difficult run with tight, rocky turns and fast, continuous rapids.

They started down the river, not wearing life jackets, helmets, or spray skirts and using plastic milk bottles for flotation. Within a short time after launching, boats and boaters were scattered all over the river. Frantic, swimming bodies tumbled into foaming holes while boats crashed into rocks and milk bottles spilled out. When the trip finally

Sjoa River in Norway

ended, only two battered kayaks remained. The other boats had been demolished. Miraculously no one suffered anything worse than bruises and scrapes, but only two of the original boaters ever kayaked again.

To avoid this kind of experience, choose rivers within your experience and ability level. Rivers are rated, according to their difficulty, on an international scale ranging from I to VI. Class I is a flat easy stretch of a river; class VI is nearly unrunnable water; and classes II, III, IV, and V have increasingly more difficult rapids. Ratings of various rivers are described in guidebooks and other sources. (The rating system is discussed in detail in the "Reading White Water" chapter.)

If you have never paddled a kayak or rowed an inflatable raft, plan to run class I water on your first trip. When you are comfortable with class I, then move on to some minor rapids of class II. Give yourself plenty of time, gaining experience on different rivers of similar difficulty before moving onto class III. Like many, you may be perfectly happy running class II or III rivers. Too often, people think in terms of ascending the white-water scale, pushing their limits to harder and harder rapids rather than simply enjoying rivers. Rapids after the class IV level present greater chances for injury or death. Unfortunately, many boaters have pushed too far too fast—some have lost friends or have had serious accidents. Many no longer boat.

If you are in white-water river running for the fun of it and are comfortable at a certain level, by all means stay with it. Most boaters run class IV rapids or lower. With good judgment and solid skills built up by beginning slowly, running this type of white water can be safe as well as exhilarating.

Information Sources

Before running a river, you will need some essential information. How difficult is the river? Are any portions of it too dangerous to run (where there is a falls, for example)? Are there any governmental rules or regulations concerning the river (that is, do you need a permit)? Is any special equipment required (fire pans or portable toilets, for example)?

Fortunately a great wealth of information exists on white-water rivers, and more is becoming available each year. Guidebooks have been published about hundreds of rivers throughout the United States, Canada, and Europe. Some of the books concentrate on a specific river while others describe many rivers within a geographical region. (If a list of guidebooks were included here, it would become outdated before this book reached the printer. That is why the "Sources" chapter includes organizations that can provide the best current lists of guidebooks, along with prices, descriptions, and ordering information.)

Special river maps are good sources of information, too. They graphically show the location of rapids, their ratings, perhaps a description of how to run the rapids, and ancillary information such as campsites, access points, and so on.

Topographic maps may be useful to you as they show the surrounding land features and various places to which your group may want to hike. For some rivers not described in guidebooks, topographic maps may be your only source of information.

The various government agencies (for example, the Forest Service, National Park Service, Bureau of Land Management, and Parks Canada) have information on the particular rivers with which they are entrusted.

Do not forget libraries. Many of them now have an inter-library loan system whereby you can request just about any book that has been published. Other sources include members of boating clubs or knowledgeable salesmen at shops carrying white-water equipment. Most likely your main source of information will be reliable boaters who have run the river.

Finally, you should be aware that guidebooks may contain wrong information about a particular river. When it comes right down to running the river, trust your judgment. If a rapid looks too hard to run, walk around it. If the river looks too high, wait a few days until it drops. The rivers always will be there for you to return to and to enjoy.

Doing It Yourself

There are several avenues available for those learning the basics of whitewater river running.

- Whether your interest is in kayaking, rafting, or canoeing white water, a number of *commercial white-water schools* can teach you basic skills. Schools are advertised and reviewed in the various periodicals concerning river running (see the "Sources" chapter). Beware of shoddy operations; check the reviews in magazines. Telephone the school and try to get a feel for their philosophy and how they run the courses. (A few schools are listed in the "Sources" chapter.)
- Some *specialized outdoor equipment shops* may sponsor occasional clinics on basic techniques.
- Most *white-water clubs* offer basic instruction for members. Pool rolling-sessions, afternoon river trips, and multi-day trips are planned by clubs. (The *American Whitewater Journal*, listed in the "Periodicals" section in the "Sources" chapter, includes a list of affiliated clubs on the back pages.)
- Some *colleges and universities* offer classes in white-water activities. For instance, Idaho State University offers three different levels of kayaking classes. Additional workshops in rowing rubber boats are offered. If there is a university near you, check its curriculum.
- Of course you can learn *on your own*. It is not the easiest way to do it, but you probably will never forget your first experiences. Instruction by professionals is the best way to begin, but help from a proficient friend may do almost as well.

I cannot emphasize enough the importance of starting on easy rivers and gradually building up your skills. Use good judgment and common sense, and you will discover a new, stimulating way of enjoying the outdoors.

Guides

Different types of guide operations are available for white-water enthusiasts. One type of service, sometimes included in the guide category, is offered by those who teach skills—how to run a raft, how to kayak, how to read water, and so on. For the purposes of this book,

Guided raft trip on section IV
of the Chattooga River in Georgia
and South Carolina

however, this type of service is classified as a white-water school (see the preceding section). Commercial services in kayaking fit into the format of these white-water schools, but differences occur in rafting services.

Two types of rafting guide operations are available: one that involves participation by guests and one that does not. On the first type of guided trip, which is common in the eastern United States, outfitters teach their guests some basic paddle strokes and everyone helps paddle the raft through rapids. On the other type of commercial guided trip, particularly many of the guide operations running multi-day trips in the western United States, the guides do most of the work, rowing rafts, cooking meals, and so on, while the guests go simply for the ride. On a few of the most expensive guided trips, extremes of comfort and luxury are the outfitter's forte. Baggage boats run ahead of the rest of the party and guides set up tents, fluff sleeping bags, and ready mixed drinks for the guests after a hard day on the river.

If you decide to begin your white-water experience with a guide, make a careful choice. A guide should help a person learn skills and learn something about the river—its moods, its delicate natural balance, and its magic. Above all, a guide should inspire his guests to help in the efforts to protect wild rivers. If you are not sure about a guide operation, consult with others who have been on the outfitter's trips or call and talk with the owner. In the end you will want to choose a guide who encourages participation in paddling or oaring a raft and is eager to help you develop the skills for organizing your own trips.

Commercial Versus Private

In the 1970s as use on rivers increased, controversy erupted, and continues today, between noncommercial (also termed "private" or "do-it-yourself" trips) and commercial users on the popular rivers of the western United States. When a great number of boaters, both non-commercial and commercial users, flocked to western rivers, land managers began to set limits on the numbers of float parties in order to protect the river environment. How many user days noncommercial and commercial parties were given often was based on historical use. For instance, on the Colorado River, allocation of use was based on the 1972 percentages of ninety-two percent commercial and eight percent non-commercial. In the years following, the Park Service, in charge of managing the Colorado River, allocated permits based on those figures.

Noncommercial use rocketed as more individuals acquired their own equipment and learned the skills to run rivers safely and inexpensively. As more noncommercial parties became interested in running the Colorado, increasing numbers of people were turned down. In 1979, 441 noncommercial parties applied to run the Grand Canyon; 394 were turned down. Noncommercial river runners were understandably upset with such an obviously biased system. Since then, the system has changed slightly, but commercial companies, by a backdoor political maneuver, managed to increase their allotment of user days. At the time of this writing, commercial user days are allocated at approximately seventy percent. Noncommercial users may have a five- to seven-year wait to get a chance to run the river. Eric Leaper of the National Organization for River Sports (Colorado Springs, Colorado) disputes the use of user days for describing the true numbers of people who run the river. If figuring use on the Colorado is based on numbers of commercial passengers as compared with numbers of noncommercial river runners, the use, according to Leaper, more closely approximates a ninety- to ten-percent split, further darkening the situation for private users on the Colorado.

Commercial operators claim they perform a valid public service. Their service is available to any member of the public who does not have the time or inclination to purchase and to run his own boat. Some commercial operators argue that they run environmentally less damaging and safer trips because of their great amount of experience.

Private river runners contend that noncommercial uses of public areas should have first priority. Many feel that commercial operators have unnaturally increased use on popular rivers by slick promotional campaigns that make rivers into a Disneyland-type experience. Oftentimes, noncommercial parties are denied access to rivers because commercial companies are given an automatic allotment, even though a commercial guide may not totally fill his trip or even run the trip.

As an alternative to present systems, organizations such as the National Organization for River Sports do not advocate the elimination of the multimillion-dollar commercial guide businesses that occur on public rivers of the West, but they do feel river managers have a responsibility to give all users—commercial and noncommercial—a fair chance to run the rivers. What is advocated instead is a reservation system, allowing a flexible allocation of use based on the demand from both the commercial and noncommercial sectors. In this system, both types of users would apply in advance to reserve a spot on the river. The more popular the river, the further in advance one would have to apply for a trip. When commercial passengers receive a date for a trip, they would then seek out an outfitter to take them down the river. A commercial guide, under the reservation system, would not be provided a fixed allocation of user days, as they are now given. Rather, he would depend on his customers' planning well in advance and making reservations with the governmental agency managing the river. Commercial guides say it is impossible for them to work under any system other than a fixed allotment, while noncommercial groups argue that the reservation system should not cause undue hardships for an aggressive and innovative operator. (For more information on this topic, a paper entitled "Allocating River Use" by Bo Shelby and Mark Danley is a good place to start and is available through the National Organization for River Sports—see "Guidebooks" section in the "Sources" chapter.)

Commercial guides involved in this issue are well organized, with extensive mailing lists and a powerful lobbying voice. Noncommercial river runners, on the other hand, are an independent lot and difficult to organize. But if noncommercial river runners are to affect any changes in river regulations that are unfair, they will have to be organized and keep current on issues. Presently, some of the best, up-to-date information that is available is found in *Currents*, a periodical published by the National Organization for River Sports (see the "Periodicals" section in the "Sources" chapter), which has taken an active role in river-related issues.

When

River water comes from three sources: snowmelt, rain, and ground-water. Man recently has introduced a fourth: water released from man-made dams. Rivers fed by snowmelt rise and fall with spring weather conditions. For example, a continuous period of eighty-degree days usually causes a dramatic peak in the river's flow. A freeze at night quickly curbs the runoff. Rivers depending on rain, of course, begin rising during a hard or a long lasting storm.

The peak runoff is the time when a particular river has its highest flow of water in a given year or season. In dry years, the peak may not represent very high water. On an average year, however, the peak usually means high water, often flowing through the brush alongside the river. Peaks are caused by melting snow or intense rainfall that imparts a surge of water to the river drainage.

How do these basic ideas help a white-water enthusiast to decide when to run a river? At certain stages of the runoff, rivers are more or less optimal for running. Often, white-water rivers at peak are too dangerous to run. The water flows through trees and bushes, places to stop are few, less time is available to make decisions, the current is powerful and less forgiving of mistakes, and the water temperature is very low. Unless you are an experienced boater and know what you are doing, a general rule of thumb is: *do not get in a white-water river that is flowing through the trees and bushes along its banks.*

The optimal time to run a river is before the peak is reached or sometime after it is past. On smaller rivers, the peak can be very dramatic and last only a few days, with a rapid decline in flow thereafter. It eventually may drop to a point where the river is too low to run later in the summer. This commonly happens on many rivers in the eastern United States or other small rivers with limited, relatively dry drainage areas. On these rivers, the season is limited to one or two months in the spring

A sign of high water and greater risks is a river flowing through trees along its banks.

during runoff or the days following a significant rainstorm. In western Canada and the western United States, with some exceptions, larger rivers with huge drainage areas have a big peak, then drop throughout the summer. Most of these rivers never drop below a point at which it is impossible to run them. On rivers such as these, it is not too much of a problem deciding when to plan your river trip. Learn when the peak time occurs, avoid it, and go any time during the remainder of the summer. For instance, July is usually an ideal month for running rivers in western North America.

The trick on smaller rivers with short seasons is to learn when those optimum times are. Good guidebooks help supply this information. The best source is boaters who run the river often.

Water Flow

The amount of water flowing down a river is measured in cubic feet per second or cubic meters per second. Flow data is collected by various governmental agencies around the world. Good guidebooks indicate the water levels that are optimal for running a particular river. For example, the best level at which to run the Rockcastle River of Kentucky is between 200 and 1500 cubic feet per second (cfs). Measured in cfs, flows around 1,000 or less indicate fairly small rivers. For a medium-sized river, flows range from approximately 1,500 to 10,000 cfs. Large rivers are considerably more. On the Colorado River, before dams were built controlling the runoff, an estimate in 1884 placed its flow at an astounding 300,000 cfs. The range of good floating levels on the Colorado is considerably less than the 1884 figure, varying from 6,000 to 24,000 cfs.

Water level information for various rivers is becoming more readily available. Newspapers in popular white-water areas publish flows of nearby rivers. Hot lines with recorded flow messages are increasingly available. For phone numbers or flow information check with white-water shops, clubs, governmental agencies managing the river, and other river enthusiasts. If the section of river lies below a dam, call up the watermaster at the dam and ask him for releases. In the United States, information about water levels may be obtained from the state offices of the United States Geological Survey and the National Weather Service. Information on the nation-wide river data system is available from the National Weather Service and Environment Canada (see the "Water Levels" section in the "Sources" chapter for addresses).

Hydrographs also are available from the previously mentioned governmental sources. A hydrograph shows in graph form the amount of water flow each day of a given year. Peaks easily can be compared from year to year, and the comparison is useful to boaters when deciding when to run a particular river.

I do not want to make it sound complicated. Most of the time you will be running rivers with accepted times for best boating; but a frequent reason for boaters getting in trouble is high water. Familiarize yourself with river flow data and make mental or written notes of how the white water changes as the level changes.

Shuttles

By the nature of things, river trips start at one point and end at another. Somehow you must get your vehicles from point to point. Arranging shuttles can be as easy as pie or as complicated as figuring out the bus schedule in a large foreign city.

Some friends and I once planned a two-week float trip. A few of the kayakers of our party were running the upper stretch of the river. The rafters flew in to a point on the river twenty-five miles below where the

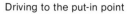
Driving to the put-in point

kayakers put in. Farther down the river at a road access, more rubber boaters were to join us. That left us with vehicles parked at three different points. We managed to work out all the logistics, but our shuttle drivers never completed the shuttle. Plagued with numerous breakdowns, they finally gave up when told by a gardener working at the Forest Service station that the river could not be run because of the fires that were "burning the canyon walls." It turned out that fires were not a major problem near the river, but all the trip money had been spent and the vehicles were barely operating, so we aborted the trip at one of the road accesses and limped home.

Shuttles can go that way sometimes. Often, getting one done is more challenging than running the river, demanding imagination and perseverance.

There are a number of ways you can do a shuttle. The easiest one is to hire a commercial shuttle driver. To obtain information on shuttle services, write to the chamber of commerce of the town near the river, check with the governmental agency in charge of the river, or stop in town and ask around.

You also can do shuttles by leaving one vehicle at one end and the other vehicle(s) at the other end. This works well if there is not too much distance involved in the shuttle and if you have plenty of time to do it. This type of shuttle can take different forms:

- Drive to the take-out point and leave one vehicle there. Everyone jumps in the other vehicle and drives to the put-in.
- If you have a motorcycle and the means to carry it on your vehicle, you can drop the cycle off at the take-out point. After you have finished your float trip, you and the other driver can ride the motorcycle back to the put-in point to retrieve the other vehicle.
- Drive to the put-in point and unload all the people and gear. Then drive the vehicles to the take-out point. Leave all but one of the vehicles at the take-out to return all drivers to the put-in. You still will need to retrieve the vehicle at the put-in.

You can do various shuttles in which the vehicles do not need to be retrieved after the float is finished:

- Drive to the put-in and unload the people and gear. Drive the vehicles around to the take-out point. All the drivers hitchhike back. This is the cheapest shuttle method and, in some unfortunate situations, can take the longest time.
- Have a friend who does not live too far from the river accompany you. Drive to the put-in and unload all the people and gear. Drive all the vehicles around to the take-out, where your friend waits for you with his own vehicle. Return to the put-in via your friend's vehicle. Then go down the river, while your friend returns home.
- Bring along extra people who are not going on the trip. These people then can drive your vehicles around to the take-out point and wait for your party to show up. Rob Lesser, who has arranged hundreds of shuttles for his many kayak trips, has these words of advice: "Many times the enjoyment of a boater's pastime requires the sacrifices of others to pull off the shuttle. Make every attempt to make the experience a positive one for the driver."

Various other methods include carrying a bicycle in the boat with you and bicycling back to the put-in point to pick up your vehicle. On short rivers with short shuttles, some people slip on a pair of shorts and dry shoes and jog back to the put-in to retrieve the vehicle.

In doing shuttles, always make it clear to the rest of the members of the group where you have put your vehicle's keys. If an accident occurs and help must be summoned, the rest of the group will need to know where the keys are. Some people bring along two sets and keep them in separate boats in case of an upset. Many river runners hide the keys on or near the vehicle so that the keys and vehicle are together. In some areas, break-ins on parked cars are a problem, so be sure to hide the keys in a safe location. Also be sure you do not accidentally leave the take-out vehicle's keys in the vehicle at the put-in. (That happened to me one rainy, cold day in the Tetons of Wyoming.)

One last note about shuttles and driving. Many people consider driving to and from the river and doing shuttles the most dangerous part of a river trip. Vehicles are heavily loaded, drivers may be tired, and everyone is itchy to get on the river. Whenever you drive, use care and caution.

Children

With careful planning and choosing of rivers, white-water boating can be enjoyed by the entire family. Rafting is the best choice for younger children on the river as they can move freely without flipping the craft, which is not possible in canoes. Older children can learn how to kayak, run a canoe, or use other inflatables. I was once on the Middle Fork of the Salmon River in Idaho in low water. Our party was slowly working its way down the river, fending off rocks and often jumping out to push rafts off shallow areas. As we scouted one rapid, a family with two rafts sailed by us. In the second raft, a fifteen-year-old boy was handling the oars better than some guides I have seen on the river.

When you bring younger children on rivers, here are some important points to keep in mind:

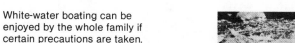
White-water boating can be enjoyed by the whole family if certain precautions are taken.

- Choose easy rivers that are at a comfortable water level and that you know well so you have no fear of capsizing a boat.
- Be sure that your own skills are very proficient and that you have a good deal of experience behind you before you bring along children.
- Teach your children from the beginning not to be afraid of water. Start them swimming at an early age and try to make those first few water experiences very positive. A bad experience may stick with them a long time.
- Let them help with repairs and general maintenance on the boats.
- Make your first trip very short. A couple of hours is fine. They will not get tired and will be excited for the next trip.
- Always have them wear life jackets. Wear yours to set a good example. Use type I, type III, or type V life jackets (see the "Day and Overnight Equipment" chapter), which provide good buoyancy and will keep a child's head upright in water, and let them learn how to fasten them. Be sure there is no way they can slip out of their life jackets. Finally, before the trip, allow them to swim in a pool with their life jackets on so they are comfortable and assured that the jackets will hold them up.

Safety

By using forethought, planning properly, and taking the right equipment, you can avoid problems, but problems do occur now and then on rivers, and the name of the game is "be prepared." If you have tried to make your trip as self-sufficient as possible, you will be in a much better situation to deal with emergencies.

When unprepared river groups get into trouble, outside help often is needed to bail them out. In many cases, a governmental agency must conduct the rescue. Most governmental agencies do not want to be in the business of rescue. Lately, internal and public pressure has been exerted on them to issue more regulations to make boating "more safe." These "safety" regulations may require that boaters use "approved" types of equipment and run certain-sized boats, and may even empower authorities to close rivers if they think the water is too dangerous. River closures usually are precipitated by accidents occurring to boaters with little or no experience or, often enough, to inner tubers. Experienced, competent river runners who can run the river relatively safely at the "closed" water levels are barred from using the river.

Two fundamental issues are important. One is that public and private authorities need to understand the difference between experienced and safe boaters as compared with inner tubers or reckless first-time paddlers. John Brown, a kayak manufacturer in Boulder, Colorado, urged in a *Currents* magazine article (May 1980) that river runners need to work with local law enforcement agencies when river closure plans are prepared in order to allow for experienced boaters. He encouraged boaters to volunteer their services to law enforcement officers during river rescues to break down some of the barriers that exist and to improve relations. Eric Leaper of the National Organization for River Sports suggests that a positive action that can be undertaken by boaters is to meet with elected officials and influential members in the county or local

Members of a fire department in the process of a river rescue. The victim, who had been trapped in the hydraulic below a small dam, survived. Some degree of risk is involved in any form of river running, but most accidents, especially this one, can be prevented by learning basic river precautions and maintaining a respect for moving water.

community and carefully explain the opportunities for river running that exist in the nearby area and some of the problems with first-time inner tubers. Often, Leaper says, elected people will be enthused about the recreational attractions in their area and may be willing to remedy existing problems.

The other fundamental issue is whether the personal safety of the boater is something that should remain an individual choice. The choice of what type of life jacket, helmet, and boat a boater should use and at what water level he feels he is competent to run a river should be left to the individual. I have encountered one river ranger at the beginning of an all kayak trip who tried to require each kayaker to carry an extra life jacket per boat to satisfy "regulations." The "regulations" of course were ridiculous. The important point, here, is that boaters should be willing to assume the responsibility for safety themselves. We live in a society where safety is regulated for us—in cities, in work, on highways, while flying on airlines—all for good reason. But on white-water rivers, we take the responsibility for safety. Too much regulation can lead us to a false sense of security—in other words, as long as we follow the regulations, we will be safe. Perhaps, but real safety cannot be put in regulations for it consists of building up our skills, preparing for river trips so we will be self-sufficient, using good equipment, walking around something we are not ready to run, and keeping a sense of respect for the river.

Rescue

Another issue related to safety is rescue. Some people feel that rescues should be free and provided by society. Others feel that outside groups should not conduct rescues. If an individual or individuals get into trouble and cannot get out of it, then he or they have to face the consequences. Other boaters feel that groups going on rivers or on wilderness trips should be prepared as much as possible, but if they find themselves in trouble and are helped by an outside rescue group, the injured should be willing to pay the full cost of the rescue. In their book *Wildwater Touring* (see the "Books" section in the "Sources" chapter), Scott and Margaret Arighi suggest that when planning trips, party members should agree at the onset of the trip that if anyone in the party is injured or becomes seriously ill, that person will burden the cost of helicopter rescue if it is needed. "The specter of high rescue cost," they note, "may instill caution in even the most reckless of individuals."

In some places rescues just are not possible. A good friend of mine, Jerry Dixon, is the river ranger for the Yukon River in the beautiful little settlement of Eagle, Alaska. A young man who was attempting to float the Yukon River downstream past Eagle into hundreds of square miles of wilderness stopped to check in with Jerry. After talking with the fellow, Jerry said it sounded like a fine trip and wished him well. "But," said the floater, "aren't you going to write anything down? Aren't you going to send someone to look for me if I don't report back?" Jerry politely explained that in that part of the United States, his agency did not have the personnel or the money to check up on people running the Yukon. Anyone doing so would have to assume the risk of injury and improbability of help.

The young man was visibly shaken and walked away. He eventually decided to continue his trip down the Yukon, but for him the trip from then on had truly become a wilderness adventure. Without the assurance of help from an outside party, he had to muster together his internal strengths and carefully undertake the venture. Jerry never learned what happened to the young man, but if his trip had been successful, it would have been a source of immense personal accomplishment, certainly far superior to a journey in which a governmental agency checked on him.

If we all go into the wilderness with a sincere effort to achieve self-sufficiency as though there were no help available, we might be able to prevent some of the increasing regulations that agencies are imposing on river runners. Safety is the responsibility and choice of individuals, and the choice is something that should be left in the wilderness experience. Let's hope that there always will be places for boaters to go where, as on the Yukon, a boater is on his own.

Protecting Rivers

Free-flowing wild rivers are in trouble. As energy and resources become more scarce, the dam builders, as they have in the past, will continue to attempt to build more dams, turning wild rivers and their white water into stagnant ponds.

If we are to protect any more rivers from the dam builders, we as boaters must get involved in the battle to help save them. Many conservation organizations are involved in fighting for wild rivers. If you are not a member of such an organization, then you should seriously consider joining one. Many free-flowing rivers still are available for white-water river running because conservation groups have worked to keep dams off them. I have met far too many river runners who use rivers, reap the benefits, and yet never lift a finger to help protect them. It does not demand too much of your time to help—only that time involved in writing a letter now and then (see the "Conservation" section in the "Sources" chapter).

On a trip I made in Hells Canyon on the Snake River on the Washington-Idaho border, we drove to the put-in place below the large Hells Canyon Dam. The power company that had financed the dam had built a neatly laid-out campground nearby, with electrical hookups, places to park trailers, and rest rooms. When we arrived, the campground beside the huge reservoir created by the dam was deserted. Below the dam, however, where the river was still flowing, there was all kinds of activity: people were hiking and fishing, and of course, we were unloading boats, getting ready to embark on a white-water trip. The people below the dam were attracted by the beauty of a dynamic, moving river, a river still living.

Loren Eiseley, the late anthropologist, once said, "If there is magic on this planet, it is contained in water…" And water that moves is particularly filled with a magic. It captures our attention and seems to invite us to mingle and dance with the flowing river. No matter what our views may be concerning how rivers are managed, let's work together to protect and save some of the magic of free-flowing rivers for ourselves now and for the children to come.

"The life of every river sings its own song…."
Aldo Leopold

RAFTS

Through the years, different types of boats have been used to challenge white-water rivers. A major, widely publicized achievement in the field was accomplished by Major John Wesley Powell when in the late 1860s, he and his party of eight others ran three, twenty-one-foot-long oak boats, and one, sixteen-foot pine boat—each vessel powered by oars and turned by a stern sweep—down the Green and Colorado rivers.

Powell, who was a scientific man, collected bits and pieces of natural information along the way. In one instance, he and his assistant, named Bradley, scaled the canyon walls to take a barometer reading to determine altitude. The climbing became difficult for the one-armed Civil War veteran. He reached up to hold onto a rock above him and suddenly found himself posed delicately on a precipitous cliff, on the verge of falling off and tumbling onto the boulders below. "The moment is critical," he wrote. "Standing on my toes, my muscles begin to tremble." Bradley scrambled above him, but was not able to obtain a close enough position to reach Powell. He frantically scanned the rocky cliffs looking for a branch of a tree to hand to Powell clinging below him, but nothing was available. Then Bradley had an idea. Pulling off his trousers, he hung them down to Powell. Powell grabbed the trousers and was pulled to safety.

The adage that small events change the course of history was proven true again. Powell might not have successfully run the wild rapids of the Colorado and explored one of the last unmapped, unknown parts of the United States had it not been for Bradley's drawers.

Powell went on a second expedition on the Colorado using boats similar to those used on the first, but this time he sat on a chair lashed to the deck and shouted orders to the oarsmen, who depending blindly on his orders, rowed with their backs to oncoming rapids (and Powell wondered why he had a hard time finding oarsmen?).

During the years after Powell's journeys, wooden boats were improved for white-water use. Metal and fiber glass dories that now are used on many western rivers are a direct outgrowth of the earlier models. Rubber rafts, then, began to appear, and especially proliferated when surplus rubber rafts were available at the end of World War II.

Rafts manufactured today are constructed of various types of synthetic materials. They come in a variety of sizes and shapes. Their distinguishing characteristic is that they are pliable but tough enough to absorb the shocks of banging and scraping against rocks without damage (most of the time, that is).

Oars versus Paddles

Inflatable rafts can be run by oars or paddles, and with or without a frame. Normally, oar boats are run with a frame constructed of wood, metal, or another material that provides a solid support for oars and a means of carrying gear. Some of the fancier frames are constructed with built-in boxes for gear storage and coolers for food.

Paddle boats are an enjoyable and exciting way of running rivers. Everyone in the raft paddles, maneuvering the boat through white water. Whether rafters should use oars or paddles, however, is one of the more controversial aspects of rafting, involving some elements of regionalism. Oar raft advocates are strongest among boaters in the western United States, while the East has many paddle advocates. If a sweeping generalization is made (of course, there are many exceptions), the differences in opinion may be due largely to what type of rafting runs are popular in an area: larger, roomier rivers of the West and smaller, tight rivers in the East. Payson Kennedy in *The All-Purpose Guide to Paddling* (see the "Books" section in the "Sources" chapter) discusses some of these differences based on his wealth of experience guiding and teaching rafting on many rivers in the East. He states that paddle boats are very effective and maneuverable on most eastern rivers and that oars in fact are "impractical" on a few rivers such as the Chattooga in South Carolina and Georgia. Conversely, B. A. Hanten, who is president of Rogue Inflatables, a raft company in Grants Pass, Oregon, and whose experience in rafting goes back many years, wrote in a recent letter: "I would defy any paddle crew to keep up with me in really picky water if I had a properly loaded raft."

It is only an overly stated generality to say that paddle boats are used in the East and oar boats are used in the West. In recent years, paddle boats have increased in popularity in the West and likewise, oars have made inroads on rivers in the East. When it comes down to what type of raft setup you use, select the one that you like the best and that works for the rivers you run.

Features

The materials, design, and other features of a raft influence how it responds in a river.

Upturned Ends. The reason for upturned ends on a raft are explained in a couple of different ways by those who are involved in the rafting industry. Ron Mattson of Cascade Outfitters, a raft supplier in Monroe, Oregon, says in material that he has prepared on raft handling characteristics that a shorter waterline length—the length of the raft that is actually in the water—enables the raft to pivot quicker. The quicker the pivoting ability, the easier the maneuvering. To achieve a short waterline length, the ends of the raft are upturned or raked.

B. A. Hanten of Rogue Inflatables, the first firm to market a raft with both ends upturned, says that the company's basic reason for using the design was not to achieve quicker pivoting, but rather to help eliminate the pressure that the current exerted on the stern while a boatman using oars ferried back and forth. Ferrying is the basic technique on which most of oar raft technique is based. As a result, the upturned end allowed the water to run under it, preventing current from piling up against the stern and improving the handling characteristics of the raft.

Richard Ford of Maravia Corporation, a manufacturer of rafts in San Leandro, California, goes along with both explanations. For oaring, Ford agrees with Hanten, advising boaters to purchase a raft with both ends upturned for easy ferrying. But for paddling, Ford recommends a boat with a medium upturn on the bow and only a slight upturn on the stern. In this way, the stern paddlers easily can reach the water to execute strokes, as can the front paddlers if they sit just aft of the upturn. Too much of an upturn in the bow, and especially the stern, prevents a paddle crew from effectively paddling.

Whether the boat is paddled or oared, its upturned bow deflects water from splashing in the raft and helps the boat ride up and over waves rather than colliding with them.

Width.   The wider the raft, the more stable it will be if it turns sideways in a rapid and is washed through a big hole. A raft with less width, however, will turn quicker and run smaller, tighter channels.

Tube Diameter.   Tube diameter determines the buoyancy of the boat. The larger the tubes the higher the boat floats, the easier it pivots, and the more gear it carries. But large tubes cut down on the amount of room in the boat and are harder to row when faced against strong winds. For paddle rafts, the tubes cannot be so large as to prevent the paddlers from reaching the water. Some general, but not necessarily absolute, guidelines on tube diameter are: for class I through III water, use a minimum tube diameter of twelve to thirteen inches; for class IV and above, use a minimum of fifteen to sixteen inches. If you generally run larger rivers with big rapids, go with larger tubes than these guidelines suggest. Tube diameters can get as large as thirty-six inches, but most boats lie in the fifteen- to twenty-two-inch range.

Materials.   Inflatable rafts are constructed of a stronger tear-resistant base fabric made of such materials as nylon, Dacron, or Kevlar. To provide resistance to abrasion, the fabric is coated with a synthetic material such as neoprene, Hypalon, neoprene-Hypalon blends, or polyvinyl chloride (PVC). It is difficult for the consumer to tell the difference in the quality of the materials used in the construction of boats since a wide variety of manufacturing processes and qualities of fabric and coating are used. Generally, price is the best guide—the more expensive the boat, the better the materials used—although a few exceptions exist, such as when a manufacturer sells directly to customers, avoiding middlemen. First learn from friends what works best for them and buy from reputable companies.

Thwarts.   Thwarts or cross tubes add lateral stability to the boat and more buoyancy. Removable thwarts generally are desirable since they allow you flexibility in using a frame and storing gear.

Chambers.   All boats used for white water should have at least two chambers on smaller crafts and four on larger. If one chamber deflates because of a bad tear, the boat then is able to remain afloat.

Valves.   Valves should be recessed, so that they are not damaged by moving gear and people getting in and out of the boat. On one cheap inflatable raft I owned, a paddling partner was thrown out in a rapid. On the way out, he scraped against a valve that was not recessed, badly lacerating his knee. Valves also should be large enough (one inch is preferred) so that a high volume of air can pass in or out, speeding up the inflation or deflation time. Military valves are a proven, reliable valve. The valve on the Avon also is good, allowing a boater to add or bleed off air

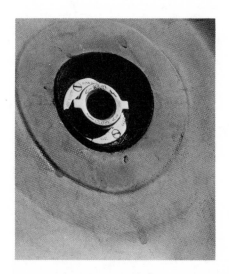

Recessed military-style valve

without unscrewing the valve.

D Rings and Other Solid Attachments. D rings glued to the sides of the tubes of a boat are used for lashing the frame and/or gear in place. The more D rings a boat has, the better. Additional D rings can be purchased from various raft distributors or made from patch material and glued to desired locations. The best rings are made of strongly welded, stainless steel, but nickle-plated rings will suffice.

Strong D rings or other solid attachments are necessary where the bow and stern ropes are tied. These lines are used for tying the raft to shore, lining it through rapids, stopping it in tight spots, and even pulling it off when it is pinned on a rock. Therefore, the ring and attachment must be solid and strong.

Size

The size of boat you use may be determined by the number of passengers you plan to carry, by the amount of gear you need to haul, or by the size of river you plan to run. For multi-day trips the amount of gear and people carried will be determining factors influencing the size of raft selected. Hanten advises that you purchase a boat large enough to carry the biggest load you anticipate. Do not go by the ratings used by some manufacturers—for example, "eight-man," "sixteen-man." These generally are the number of people that can be crammed into a life raft in an emergency on the ocean, and have no application to white water.

The "Determining Raft Size" chart will help you determine the number of people the raft will comfortably hold for paddling or oaring. The figures allow for the additional weight of carrying equipment for a week-

Determining Raft Size

Length of Raft	Width of Raft	Paddle Boat Maximum Number of People	Oar Boat Maximum Number of People
8 to 10 feet (2.4 to 3.1 meters)	4 to 5 feet (1.2 to 1.5 meters)	2	1
11 to 12 feet (3.4 to 3.7 meters)	5 to 6 feet (1.5 to 1.8 meters)	3 or 4	2
12 to 13 feet (3.7 to 4.0 meters)	5 to 6 feet (1.5 to 1.8 meters)	4	2 or 3
13 to 14 feet (4.0 to 4.3 meters)	6 feet to 6 feet 8 inches (1.8 to 2.0 meters)	4 or 6	3
14 to 16 feet (4.3 to 4.9 meters)	6 feet 8 inches to 8 feet (2.0 to 2.4 meters)	6 or 8	3 or 4
16 to 18 feet (4.9 to 5.5 meters)	7 feet 6 inches to 8 feet (2.3 to 2.4 meters)	8	5 or 6

long trip. The smaller rafts listed must carry lightweight-style equipment and food, while the larger rafts can carry heavy, luxurious-style gear if desired. The figures are only approximate. You may want to add or subtract people to accommodate your situation better. For instance, Ron Mattson of Cascade Outfitters suggests adding one to three people in lieu of baggage on day trips and Reg Lake of River Touring Equipment suggests adding one more person to the paddle boats to act as "captain" in the stern.

Care

Rafts made of synthetic materials are tough and can withstand a lot of abuse, but observing the following points will help prolong their life:

- Be careful when traveling to and from the river. Pad the raft so that in transit it will not vibrate against any sharp objects. Some friends of mine borrowed my brand new raft and treated it like a baby on their river trip, but upon returning, the boat rubbed against the side of their trailer, wearing a hole in the tube. Keep the boat in a heavy sack while traveling.
- Keep the boat clean while on the river. Sponge out sand and pebbles, which can grind away in the corners of the raft's floor.
- At the end of the trip give the raft a good washing. Allow it to dry and pack it away.
- Store the boat in a dry, cool area, dusting it with talcum powder to help it stay dry. Avoid piling other heavy items on it. Some manufacturers recommend storing their boats half inflated if storage space is available.

Frameless Oar Rafts

This topic elicits as many pro and con comments from boaters as the issue of paddles versus oars. A frameless oar raft is one that does not use a wood or metal frame as a base for oarlocks and gear storage. The oars are placed through a rubber or metal oarlock coupled with the tube of the raft via an oarlock mount. Advocates of the frameless system point out its simplicity and light weight in situations where portages must be made. If the raft capsizes, no heavy unyielding frame can come down on top of the rafters.

Those who feel that frameless oar rafts are a poor choice for rafting claim that the rubber oarlocks or other oarlock systems that depend on the tube of the raft for support are too flimsy for positive rowing and that without a frame, gear storage is greatly complicated. It also is argued that on multi-day trips, rafters carry a number of hard objects, which can injure rafters as well as frames can if the raft capsizes.

Other rafters do feel the frameless setup works and use it. I was on a Colorado River trip with two rafters who rowed without frames using Avon oarlocks. Other friends have used them on rivers where several portages were necessary. Another group plans to use frameless Maravia rafts with oars for exploratory rafting in Nepal.

If you decide to try frameless boats, two factors are important: a stiff boat, such as a Maravia or an Avon, and a good oarlock system. Avon has a synthetic rubber oarlock, which can be purchased separately and

This synthetic rubber Avon oarlock has been altered for white-water use. Tying webbing or rope between two holes drilled in opposite sides of the oarlock prevents the oar from popping out.

cemented on other rafts. For white water, a slight alteration should be made in the Avon oarlock by drilling two holes and tying a rope or strap between them to keep the oar from popping out. The Maravia oarlock system needs no adjustments for white-water use as it has a metal oarlock held by a synthetic base attached to the raft.

Carrying Gear on Frameless Rafts. If you decide not to use any type of frame for either an oar or paddle raft, you will need to devise ways of tying gear so that it does not sit directly on the bottom of the boat, a chief cause of ripped floors. If you are going on a multi-day trip, gear storage becomes an acute problem, but various methods exist, including the following:

Tying gear on frameless rafts. To avoid ripped floors, gear is tied to tubes by lines strung through D rings.

- Glue D rings on the inside and outside of the bow of the raft. Set gear bags on top of the tube and run lines back and forth between the D rings to hold the bags securely in place. Reg Lake of River Touring Equipment suggests that tight straps around the thwarts make good points for attaching lines.
- Place an inner tube or tough air mattress on the bottom of the boat. Lash the gear together, pile it on top, and tie it to D rings on the side of the boat so it stays in place.
- Some boaters move the thwarts, tie them together, and use them for a base on which to tie gear.
  String a net made of nylon cord or webbing across the boat. Place the gear in the net, then suspend it above the floor of the boat.

There are many different ways of attacking the problem of tying gear above the floor, and at times, it will take experimentation and revision until you come up with the best system for you. The frameless raft is light, simple, and much safer in an upset than a raft with a frame. The important thing is to ensure that the lashing system you use suspends the gear off the floor and is tied so that the gear will not fly against passengers if the boat flips. In addition, it is extremely important to tie off all lines and be sure that there is no way that you or your boat mates' feet can become entangled in lines. Loose lines wrapped around legs are one of the most dangerous hazards to river runners.

Paddle Raft Frame

For multi-day trips, some paddlers build a small square frame to fit in the middle of the raft to hold gear. In this way, most of the weight is placed in the middle of the boat, making it easier to turn. Construction of the frame is easy. Just lay two-by-six boards on top of the tubes and cut them so they fit your boat, or use a metal frame. To form a net to suspend the gear off the floor, you can tack webbing on or tie it into holes drilled in the wood or tie it to the metal.

Frame to hold gear for multi-day paddle raft trips

Wood Oar-Raft Frames

For oar rafts, several types of wood frames can be constructed easily. The advantage of wood is that it is inexpensive when compared with commercially available frames and you can easily build a frame out of it. If you decide to go with wood, the wood oar frame photographs will give you an idea of how the frame goes together. If you would like to delve

Wood oar frame with suspension net in middle

Wood oar frame with side walls

deeper into the art of building frames, the best source—complete with plans—is William McGinnis's fine book *Whitewater Rafting* (see the "Books" section in the "Sources" chapter).

As you build a wooden frame, there are a few points to keep in mind. Two-by-six boards of pine or fir are adequate. For more strength and comfort when sitting but also more weight, you can use two-by-eight or wider boards. The length of the boards depends on your boat. Inflate the boat and set the boards on top of the tubes. Cut the seat boards to fit across the raft. Before assembling the frame, lay all boards in place and be sure everything fits. Use carriage bolts to bolt the boards together. Do not bolt the oarsman's seat until after the oarlock mounts are in place.

Recess the bolts so they do not protrude beyond the edge of the wood. Any exposed bolt can cause damage to the boat or injury to a person who scrapes across it. To prevent wear, glue carpet to the bottom of the boards on top of the tubes.

Oarlock mounts (see a later section in this chapter) can be purchased from rafting suppliers. Mount them on the boards sitting on top of the tubes so that they are located in the middle of the raft or just a few inches toward the rear. The middle of the board on which the oarsman sits should be mounted sixteen to twenty-one inches behind the oarlocks. Before actually bolting the oarsman's seat, put the oars in place and sit on the seat to be sure the arrangement feels comfortable for oaring.

Metal Oar-Raft Frames

Metal frames are now the most commonly used frame on an oar raft. They are strong, light, and available in models that break down for transporting to and from the river. Constructed of steel and aluminum tubing, a wide variety of models is now marketed by raft supply companies. As part of the frame design for gear storage, various styles incorporate large coolers for seats, boat boxes, or tables. Customizing of metal frames is possible through various companies that sell them, or you can design your own metal frame and have a welder close to home do the work.

Metal oar frame

Additional Gear Storage Hints

For either wood or metal frames, there are a few additional points to consider.

To provide additional carrying capacity, you can hang pieces of plywood, cut to fit, on the inside of the boat. These "floorboards" can be

Floorboards on wood oar frame. Inner tubes can be inflated and tied to the bottom of the floorboard to keep them supported above the floor of the raft.

hung with webbing affixed to the frame or to D rings on the side of the boat. Coolers, boat boxes, and other gear can be set on the boards. Check the floorboards from time to time while on the river. They sometimes can work down and sit directly on the bottom, making the floor very vulnerable to rips. To help give the boards extra support, some boaters inflate inner tubes and tie them to the underside of the boards, or as Ron Mattson suggests, you can fasten ethafoam, available from river supply companies, to the bottom of the boards using contact cement. If you use floorboards, remember to leave an area open so you can bail out the boat.

Since everything you carry should be suspended off the floor and tied in place, loading and unloading boats can take time. Anything that is built into the frame that will make the loading and unloading process easier will save time on the river.

Using nylon straps with buckles is less time-consuming than tying and untying knots. Various types of clips, such as carabiners used by mountain climbers, can be used to get equipment on and off easily.

I use a large open bag made out of heavy-duty nylon for storing all kinds of gear, large or small—large duffle bags of personal gear, Dutch ovens, buckets, and so on. It clips onto a middle section of my frame, with a net of nylon webbing below it providing extra support for the bag. The top folds over, and all the gear is securely held in place with a couple of straps.

Some boaters pile gear on a suspended floorboard and throw a canvas or heavy-duty tarp over the gear. The tarp is clipped down and a series of ropes or straps laced over the top to lash everything down securely. A white canvas tarp is particularly useful over food containers, since on hot days, a damp, white tarp keeps food cool.

Oarlocks and Oarlock Mounts

The different types of oarlocks have their advocates. Basically, most of the strong pro and con comments center on the U-shaped oarlocks and tholepins.

U-Shaped Oarlocks. Also called oar horns, open oarlocks, or

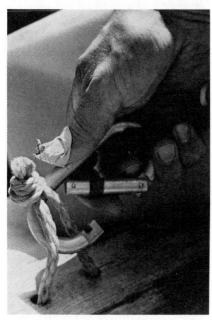

A carabiner is used to clip gear on the raft.

simply oarlocks, U-shaped oarlocks are constructed of bronze, manganese, silver bronze, or other materials. They allow the oars to be rotated or to be pulled in and out of the lock. One of the chief arguments in favor of them is offered by B. A. Hanten, who says that they allow the oar to be rolled slightly while being pulled through the water. The rolling of the oar changes the pitch of the blade so it gets a full bite of water as it travels in an arc with each stroke, giving the rower the most power for energy expended. Hanten describes it as being similar to adding a turbocharger to an automobile. He adds that the tholepin system, with its fixed position, is oriented in the correct position for a blade full of water or maximum power for a very small portion of the stroke, making it less efficient. Because the U-shaped oarlocks are flexible and allow oars to pop out of the oarlocks when under a great amount of stress, many boatmen feel they are safer.

U-shaped oarlock and mount

U-shaped oarlocks slip into oarlock mounts or sockets bolted to the frame of the boat. They are available commercially.

Tholepins and Clips.   This oarlock system consists of a pin or heavy shaft of metal mounted on the frame. A clip is attached to the oar and clipped on the pin for rowing. The advantage of this system, according to advocates, is that it keeps the oar fixed in place as strokes are made. With U-shaped oarlocks, an oarsman always must keep a tight grip on the handles and be sure the oar blade is correctly oriented. That is not the case with tholepins and thus, they are a good choice, advocates recommend, for people learning how to oar. So once again, the choice of which type of equipment to use is a personal preference.

Other Systems.   Other oarlock systems are available, including round oarlocks, clamped-on types, and various other improvisations, but the U-shaped oarlocks and tholepin systems are the most common.

Oars

Wood or Synthetic.   Both synthetic and wood oars are available. The best wood oars are straight-grained ash oars. Check for knots, which weaken the oar. Wood oars demand extra care and for protection should be coated with a marine oil or exterior varathane. The handle, however, should not be coated in order to provide a good gripping surface. The shaft of a wood oar needs to be protected because it rubs against the oarlock. Various materials can be wrapped around the shaft, including nylon cord (3/16 braided), leather, or webbing.

Tholepin and clip oaring setup

Synthetic oars are available and now have surpassed wood in strength. They usually consist of a plastic blade with a metal shaft covered with a plastic sleeve. Some models have interchangeable blades in different widths, which are convenient if a blade is broken. Though the synthetic oar offers advantages, some boaters still prefer wood because, like a good cross-country ski, a wood oar has a comfortable, aesthetic feel.

Oar Stops.   Oar stops are necessary if you utilize the U-shaped oarlock. Without them, the oar easily could slip off and fall into the river. The exact location of an oar stop depends on personal preference. Some like to position it just below the handle grip, while others position it just above where the oarlocks encircle the oar shaft.

Oar Length.   Pat Agidius of Northwest River Supplies (Moscow, Idaho) points out that oar size generally is based on the width of the raft. A general rule for determining oar length is that one-third the length of an oar should fall between your hand and an oarlock. Agidius notes that the "ideal" is not always wanted and there are other factors, such as comfort, the weight of the load, and personal preference, that enter into the decision. The "Determining Oar Size" chart will give you a general idea of the size of the oar you may choose to match your boat.

Paddles

Wood or Synthetic.   Many different types of paddles are available for rafters in paddle boats. Many boaters prefer the comfort, warmth, and aesthetics of wood. Wood paddles normally are constructed of laminated combinations of hard and soft woods. For white water, paddles that have blades reinforced with fiber glass are advisable. The disadvantages of

Synthetic oars

Oar stops are positioned according to personal preference. Some boaters place them near the handle while others have them riding just above the oarlock.

Determining Oar Size

Boat Length	Oar Length
8 to 10 feet (2.4 to 3.1 meters)	6 to 7 feet (180 to 210 centimeters)
11 to 12 feet (3.4 to 3.7 meters)	7 to 8 feet (210 to 240 centimeters)
12 to 13 feet (3.7 to 4.0 meters)	8 to 10 feet (240 to 310 centimeters)
13 to 14 feet (4.0 to 4.3 meters)	9 to 10 feet (270 to 310 centimeters)
14 to 16 feet (4.3 to 4.9 meters)	9 to 10 feet (270 to 310 centimeters)
16 to 18 feet (4.9 to 5.5 meters)	10 to 12 feet (310 to 370 centimeters)

wood paddles are that they require additional maintenance and are weaker than good synthetic paddles.

Synthetic paddles are made from various types of fiber glass resins and plastics. Those with metal shafts are among the strongest. Vinyl esters, epoxies, and Kevlar cloth materials are expensive but virtually unbreakable. Less expensive synthetic paddles are constructed by injecting plastic into a mold (referred to as injection molded). The blades are attached to an aluminum shaft. Some worthless injection molded paddles are found on the market, but if bought from reputable paddle companies, this type of paddle is a reasonable choice for white water. The best grip for white-water use is a T grip. The T shape provides a good hold for paddlers in the forceful currents of rapids.

Length. The length of a paddle for white-water rafting will fall in the 4- to 6-foot (120- to 180-centimeter) range. Actual size depends on the height of the person using the paddle and the size of the tubes on the raft. The ideal size is determined by sitting on the tube of the boat. As you begin to paddle, the top hand on the grip of the paddle should be at nose level while the paddle blade is immersed totally in the water for a stroke. The stern paddler in a raft may opt for a slightly longer paddle since he may be making wide, sweeping strokes.

T grips are best for white-water paddlers.

Pumps

Two types of pumps are available: a foot bellows pump, which requires little expenditure of energy since the leg muscles are used, and a barrel pump. A barrel pump involves a little more work, but moves a greater volume of air. If you choose a barrel pump, go with a large-volume type that has a barrel with a 5½-inch diameter and an 18-inch length. The bigger it is, the better because it will move more air in less time than smaller pumps. Also, electric pumps that plug into car lighters for quick inflation are available. But always carry a manual pump for use in repairs or for tightening up the boat while you are on the river.

Barrel pump (*left*) and foot bellows pump (*right*)

Waterproof Bags

The style of your trip may determine the type of waterproof gear-storage containers you use. If you are going on a luxurious-style trip, heavy gear bags are not too much of a problem. You may use heavy wood boxes, fiber glass containers, and bulky, metal ammo cans. But if you are traveling light or just do not like messing with heavy containers, you will want to use soft, waterproof bags.

Various vinyl and polyethylene bags are available on the market. Some are cheap and usually are ready to be disposed of after the first trip. Others are expensive and well made. If you decide to use vinyl or polyethylene bags, select those that are covered with a nylon outer bag to protect them from punctures and tears. These types of bags, nonetheless, are delicate, and many boaters prefer to go to a stronger, longer lasting bag.

Some of the best, soft, waterproof bags are constructed of materials similar to those used in inflatable rafts. These bags, available commercially, are constructed of PVC-covered Dacron, Hypalon, or other materials. You can construct one yourself by buying a large piece of raft repair

Vinyl bag with a roll-down,
snap-shut closure

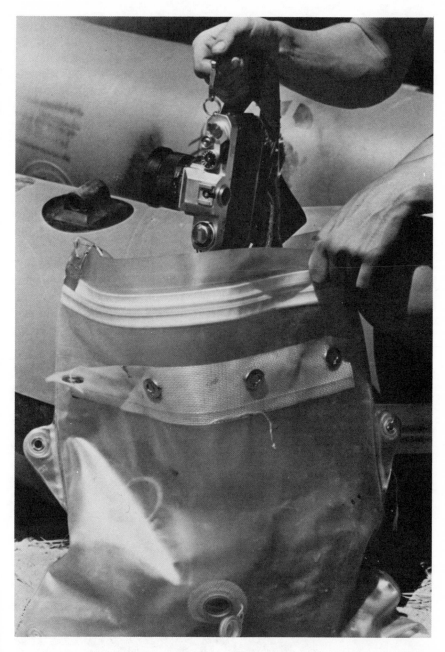

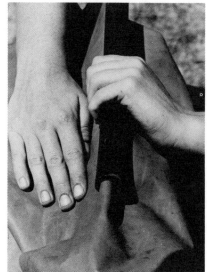

Putting a slide closure in place

material or similar material and gluing the sides together, leaving an open top. After you pack gear inside, seal the top with a plastic clamp (see the next paragraph), which can be made or purchased from a supply house.

On any type of waterproof bags, the closure is the weak link in the system. One reliable method of sealing the bag is to use a slide closure. (One source of slide closures is Voyageur's, listed in the "Equipment" section in the "Sources" chapter.) I use slide closures on certain fold-over-and-strap-down tops that were supposed to be waterproof. Slide closures can pop off under pressure, but can be secured by using inner tube bands, described later in this section. Other systems include roll-down-and-snap-shut, zippered, and tied tops. Unfortunately, a number of bags on the market are a farce. They may be advertised as "waterproof," but in reality they allow water to leak in, usually through the closure. The best test for any bag is to fill it with water, close the top, and tip it upside down. Not even a drip of water should appear. If it does, send it back to the company or take it back to the store. This unnecessary leakage is unsuitable for white-water use. If you put money into a waterproof bag, and most are expensive, you should be assured it will not leak. I once bought a new waterproof bag with a roll-down top. After a day of normal splashing, I opened the bag to find my belongings, including three books, soaked.

A cheap storage method, if money is tight and you have barely enough to pay for gas to get to the river, is to use thick plastic garbage bags. Put two garbage bags inside a duffle bag or rucksack. Stuff your gear in the inside garbage bag, packing hard items inside soft items to prevent tears. Squeeze all the air out of the inside garbage bag. Tie it off with a clove hitch. Then tie off the outside garbage bag with another clove hitch. Use the duffle bag or rucksack on the outside to keep the bags from ripping.

On certain types of waterproof bags, especially those that roll down, you can use a loop from an inner tube to help keep the bag rolled tight and sealed. Make two cuts through an inner tube so that you make a large rubber band one-half- to three-quarters-inch thick. Wrap this around the rolled up closure several times to get a secure seal. The inner tube band

A.

B.

A clove hitch is used to tie off a plastic garbage bag being used for waterproof storage (*A*). The bag then is placed inside another plastic bag, placed inside a duffle or nylon bag, and tied off with another clove hitch (*B*) before the outermost duffle or nylon bag is sealed.

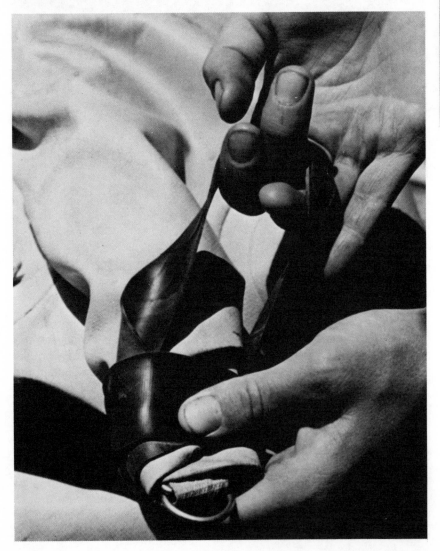

An inner tube band is a handy way to keep a bag tightly sealed.

is quick and easy. Bring extras along as they can be used for other purposes as well.

One final hint: Before closing a waterproof bag, encircle it with your arms and push out all the air. Sometimes it helps to close the top partially, then push as much air out as possible. The bag should look drawn and sucked in. Quickly close the bag completely. This procedure helps relieve the pressure on the bag material and its seams and makes it easier to lash down.

Rigid Waterproof Containers

The most common and most widely available rigid, waterproof containers are those used to carry ammunition, often called ammo cans. Some boaters use sealed wood boxes; others use fiber glass boxes. All these containers are heavy. For lighter weight, waterproof plastic boxes are available in different sizes—smaller ones for carrying cameras, first aid items, or repair supplies and larger ones for carrying bulkier items. They often are advertised in river magazines (see the "Periodical" section in the "Sources" chapter).

When you buy rigid waterproof containers, carefully examine the opening. To prevent water from leaking inside, the opening should be clamped down against a gasket. You can use the same test for waterproofness on rigid containers as is used on soft containers. Fill the container with water, seal it, and turn it upside down. No water should leak from the lid. This test is particularly important with rigid containers since they may be used for valuable items, such as cameras and binoculars.

Rigid containers should have strong tie-on points to make them easier to lash to the raft. Strong handles should be provided on larger containers to aid in moving them on and off the raft when they are filled with heavy gear.

A cheap alternative for rigid storage containers are large, five-gallon plastic containers that are used for food items such as mayonnaise. You may be able to acquire these from restaurants or school or hospital food service operations. The containers have leak-proof lids and are ideal for keeping gear and food dry.

Rigid waterproof containers: plastic box (*left*) and ammo can (*right*)

Dory

Dories and McKenzie Boats

Long before inflatable rafts were available, wood dories were used by river runners tackling white-water rivers. No chapter on river craft would be complete without mentioning them. River dories closely resembling the North Sea fishermen's dory have been adapted to meet the demands of white water. Constructed of wood, aluminum, or fiber glass, dories are beautiful, maneuverable, hard-hulled boats. Because of their comfort and aesthetics, they are the Cadillac of white-water craft, but due to the unforgiving nature of the materials used in building them (as compared with rafts), boatmen who run dories must have a high degree of skill. (See the "Inflatable Rafts and Dories" chart for a subjective comparison of rafts and dories. Its primary purpose is to present a general idea of the differences among them.)

The McKenzie boat, developed on the McKenzie River in Oregon, is an example of one particular style of dory and is functionally oriented to fly fishing. The boat is constructed so that a fisherman can stand and brace himself in the front of the boat and lay his line on a special lining deck. The boat is highly maneuverable and, with a skilled boatman, can run surprisingly rocky, technical white water. Other styles of dories include larger, decked-over models, which are used in big white water such as that found on the Colorado River.

Sources of Rafts, Dories, and Other Equipment

Any equipment and boats mentioned in this book are available from selected companies listed in the "Equipment" section in the "Sources" chapter.

Inflatable Rafts and Dories

Type of Craft	Advantages	Disadvantages
Inflatable Oar Raft	Can carry a large amount of gear. Comfortable. Good for use with children. Unskilled passengers can ride. When used with certain types of frames, the ride can be fairly dry through splashing rapids.	No group participation. Can have difficulty in certain types of small rocky rivers. If frames are used, more chance of injury if boat capsizes.
Inflatable Paddle Raft	Everyone participates. Good choice for small, shallow, rocky rivers. Some very effective, complicated maneuvering can be carried out by a well-trained paddle crew. Some amount of leaning and bracing can be done in executing eddy turns and preventing capsizing in holes.	Commands to maneuver boats must be relayed to all paddlers, slowing reaction times. Rides are wetter and for some people, uncomfortable. For difficult white water, the paddle crew needs to work together and practice in advance.
Dories	A luxury class of river craft. More maneuverable than inflatable rafts. Seats with cushions and back rests. Dry. Aesthetically pleasing. McKenzies, a type of dory, are the best boats for fishing.	Boatman must be highly skilled. Boats are more easily damaged than inflatable rafts. Repair is more difficult. Limited amount of gear can be carried. Some heavier dories are not suited for shallow, rocky water.

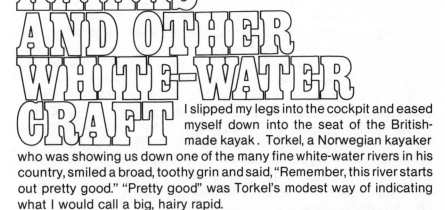

KAYAKS AND OTHER WHITE-WATER CRAFT

I slipped my legs into the cockpit and eased myself down into the seat of the British-made kayak. Torkel, a Norwegian kayaker who was showing us down one of the many fine white-water rivers in his country, smiled a broad, toothy grin and said, "Remember, this river starts out pretty good." "Pretty good" was Torkel's modest way of indicating what I would call a big, hairy rapid.

I was having grave doubts about the sanity of this broad-shouldered, smiling Norwegian. We already had heard some chilling tales about destroyed boats and aborted trips on the Sjoa River (pronounced "Shew-ah"), which tumbles out of the glaciated Jotunheimen mountainous region of central Norway. When I had first met Torkel at a Norwegian railway station, we had talked about a trip that he had taken to the United States a few years before. While there, he had parachuted off the sheer face of El Capitan in Yosemite National Park. The fact that he had jumped off a cliff three thousand feet above the valley floor did not do much to ease my nervousness as we pushed off.

Torkel was not kidding. The first rapid that rushed out of sight from the put-in point was obstructed by boulders and holes and demanded quick maneuvers. The river narrowed and dropped through several large curling-back holes. At the first break in the rapid in a small calm spot, Barney, my boating companion from the States, washed in behind us upside down, attempting several rolls and finally coming up before the next series of rapids, which splashed out of sight around the bend.

The river continued its fast pace, with narrow chutes, boulder fields, and drops into holes. My reservations about Torkel faded as I watched him smoothly and cautiously gliding back and forth, searching out eddies and stopping safely above major rapids that needed scouting. The river allowed kayaking at its best, with lots of maneuvers, continuous white water along the river's entire length, and good places to stop to scout ahead. The water was clear, pure enough to drink, and at times felt like champagne bubbles as we paddled through it. Waterfalls spilled over the canyon walls and lush verdant moss and vegetation clung to the polished boulders along the shore.

The maneuverable kayak and its relative, the decked canoe or C-1, are the types of craft that make it possible to experience rivers like Norway's Sjoa. Years ago, to the south of Norway in Europe, the North American Eskimo kayak was adapted and found to be superbly maneuverable in the shallow, rocky streams characteristic of the Continent. Now, well-constructed kayaks made of different types of fiber glass, resins, and strong plastics are used to challenge all types of white-water rivers throughout the world.

Kayaks and Decked Canoes

The white-water kayak has gone through a number of evolutions since the days when it was an Eskimo skin boat, sealed by the user's parka and utilized for hunting. Much of the development of the kayak, occurring in Europe, produced a boat that is the lightest and the most maneuverable of white-water craft. Kayaks are classified as either K-1, which is a kayak for one person, or K-2, which is a kayak for two people.

Also as maneuverable as the K-1 is the decked canoe or C-1. The canoeist kneels and uses a single-bladed paddle while the kayaker sits with legs extended under the deck and uses a double-bladed paddle. A canoe is slightly larger and more buoyant than a kayak. Both are constructed with a rim around the cockpit on which a spray skirt can be attached, completely sealing out water. With a special technique, both crafts can be rolled back to an upright position if they are knocked over in white water. (See the "Kayaks and Decked Canoes" chart for a generalized comparison of the two boats.)

C-1 or decked canoe

Kayaks and Decked Canoes

	Advantages	Disadvantages
White-Water Kayak (K-1)	Quick, maneuverable, and able to run the most technical of white water. Can be rolled upright in an upset. Can run very shallow, small rivers and streams. Efficient paddling with a double-bladed paddle. Good bracing ability on both sides to prevent flips. Lower center of gravity providing greater dynamic stability than a canoe.	At first, the kayak is unstable, and a beginner may take some swims. Seats can be cramped and uncomfortable. Remote possibility of legs becoming entrapped if boat is pinned. Boater sits lower than in a C-1, and thus the kayaker cannot see so much while on the river.
White-water Decked Canoe (C-1)	Good transition for boaters who previously have used open canoes. Higher than a kayak; thus one can see more in rapids. Little danger of becoming pinned under the deck because of the kneeling position. Larger volume than kayak; carries more gear. Good boat for large boaters. Very strong bracing and powerful strokes on the paddling side.	At first, the C-1 is unstable and swims can be expected by a beginner. Paddling is done on one side, leaving the other side vulnerable; more difficult to keep upright than a kayak if tipped in that direction. Forward paddling less efficient than with a kayak.

Kayak Design

Volume. Volume as explained by Tom Derrer, a boat designer for Eddyline Northwest (Everett, Washington), in an article in *Canoe* magazine (November 1980), is an indication of how much weight a kayak adequately can carry and gives an approximate idea of its buoyancy. Rob Lesser, who has made a number of first descents of extremely difficult rivers, recommends that a kayaker in the 180- to 200-pound range use a larger-volume, more buoyant boat. A heavy kayaker makes a less buoyant boat ride lower in the water than it should, making the boat lose some of the handling characteristics it was designed for. Ken Horwitz of Perception, a kayak manufacturer in Liberty, South Carolina, recommends large-volume kayaks for multi-day trips where gear-storage space is needed and for beginning kayakers who need a more stable boat when first learning. Dick Held of Whitewater Boats, a kayak manufacturer in Cedar City, Utah, says, "Larger volumes usually draw less water and sink less, making them a good choice for small streams or shallow ledges."

Buoyancy, however, is not simply a function of volume. New designs, as Horwitz explains, have changed hull design and deck-to-hull distances, creating relatively buoyant, but low-volume, highly maneuverable kayaks. Many good kayakers running big water rivers feel that the extra maneuverability is an important safety factor.

Manufacturers and product reviews, such as those periodically run in *Canoe*, rate kayaks according to low, medium, and high volumes, giving prospective buyers an idea of how much space is available inside. If you have the opportunity, by all means try different boats and select the one that works best for you.

Rocker.   If the hull of a kayak is viewed from the side, a wide arch is outlined beginning at the bow and curving down to the ground and back up to the stern. This curvature is called *rocker*. On a simplistic level, the more rocker a boat has, the less the ends drag in the water and the easier it is to turn. It is possible to go overboard with too much rocker, but all white-water kayaks are designed with a reasonable amount of rocker to enable them to maneuver adequately in rapids.

Length and Width.   The width on many boats conforms to standards set by an international racing committee. The minimum for kayaks is 60 centimeters (23.6 inches) and for C-1s is 70 centimeters (27.6 inches). The committee also sets the length, which for a kayak is 4 meters (13.1 feet). New innovations in design have led to kayaks with different dimensions, especially shorter lengths. Though these shorter boats (sometimes called *play-boats*) are not the type of kayak for every boater, they are making an impact on the market.

Other Design Features.   Different types of kayakers prefer different designs for their personal style and the type of rivers they run. Rob Lesser recommends a kayak with a low-cut cockpit area. This allows the kayaker greater mobility for leaning, bracing, and rolling than a cockpit that is higher. Lesser thinks the low cockpit is particularly important in the type of roll he advocates in which a boater lies back against the rear deck of the kayak at the conclusion of the roll (see the "Kayak Technique" chapter).

One design feature the Europeans are using is a blunt, sharply upturned bow of the kayak. This is a safety feature designed to prevent the dangerous situation of entrapping the bow of the kayak between boulders on the bottom of the river when dropping over steep drops (see the "Safety" chapter).

Choosing a Kayak for Your Needs.   By using different shapes of hulls and decks, boat designers can create kayaks to fulfill radically different requirements. For instance, kayaks for downriver racing (also called wild-water racing) are sleekly designed with typically deep V–shaped hulls and little, if any, rocker. Kayaks also are designed for white-water slalom racing, sea cruising, and other purposes. But for recreational white-water use, which this book is all about, there are two categories that will be of importance to boaters: white-water play-boats and white-water touring kayaks.

Derrer explains that *white-water play-boats* are shorter boats with varying designs, which are ideally suited for surfing and playing in waves and holes in rapids. Many kayakers are using these boats for river running and, as mentioned previously, they are gaining acceptance. *White-water touring kayaks* for years have been, and will continue to be, an excellent boat for white water. With volumes in the medium and high ranges, they are good for day outings and can carry extra gear for overnight or multi-day kayaking.

Some people who plan to run minor white water and flat rivers or lakes may be interested in *casual recreation boats*. These boats can run, though sluggishly, up to class III white water. *White-water slalom racing boats* also should be briefly mentioned. They are designed so specifically

With different hull and deck shapes, kayaks can be designed to perform radically different functions.

for slalom racing and thus are so small and unstable that a recreational boater will be much better off staying with either the play-boat or white-water touring boat.

Kayak Materials

White-water kayaks are manufactured using a number of different materials. One of the common materials is fiber glass cloth (also called E glass) combined with vinyl ester resin. Each manufacturer of fiber glass kayaks takes pride in offering boats with specific reinforced areas, which he has determined because of his own experience. Some use nylon layers between the fiber glass and the deck. Any reputable boat builder has reasons for his particular design and each design has merit since it comes from a designer who also is an active paddler.

Another form of fiber glass, Kevlar, is so light that bulletproof vests are fabricated from it. It is very expensive and found on kayaks used for competition or by devoted kayakers who strive to get maximum strength per weight.

Recently, rotationally molded polyethylene kayaks have made a hugh impact on the recreational market. While heavier than competition-weight fiber glass kayaks, they are more durable and rarely need to be repaired. In the past, serious paddlers were reluctant to switch to plastic boats (as a few boaters still are), but now that the boats have improved designs and safety systems, many expeditionary kayakers have proven their worth on the difficult rivers of the world.

The basic bone of contention of the plastic versus fiber glass issue is that if the kayak is broached and wrapped on a rock, a fiber glass boat will break, allowing the paddler to get out, while a plastic model will collapse, entrapping the paddler. To prevent entrapment, foam walls or pillars are placed in the kayak. Pillars, however, are not total insurance that the boat will not collapse. Mike Snead of the Sierra Kayak School (Lotus, California) has seen an entrapment with the pillars in place. The kayak bent between the front and back pillars at the seat area. The entrapped boater was rescued successfully, but Snead changed to a pillar system using a six-foot-long fiber glass shaft along the bottom of the boat, from under one pillar to under the other, to prevent a recurrence. Various other systems are being tested, but it would be misleading to say a fail-safe system has been developed.

However, plastic-boat advocates counter by saying that many glass manufacturers have pushed fiber glass technology to the point that many glass boats are too strong to crack like an egg in a broach. Various breakaway cockpits are designed into fiber glass boats and some, such as the Phoenix of Phoenix Products (Tyner, Kentucky), have worked in real entrapment situations. Dick Held of Whitewater Boats combines a breakable fiber glass deck with an ABS/Royalex hull. Despite these fiber glass designs, they do not ensure safety.

All this talk about entrapment may lead you to think that it is an overriding fear of kayakers. On the contrary, most boaters using care on rivers will never experience it. Perception, a major plastic-boat manufacturer, reminds boaters to follow the acceptable safety practice of leaning into a rock. If for any reason the boat begins to get caught and tipped upstream or begins to wrap, the kayaker should bail out immediately.

The arguments over what is the best and safest type of kayak are sure to go on for a number of years. Very good arguments are made for both sides and the final choice is up to the individual kayaker.

Bracing and Features

Foot Braces. Every kayak should have foot braces, which are usually two small pedals mounted on each side inside the boat to enable the boater to brace himself securely. Foot braces that can be adjusted by a spring-loaded lever are by far the best. Poorly designed braces are those that adjust by pins or screws and require a boater to crawl headfirst into the cramped kayak, usually going through numerous contortions to try to adjust them. Avoid an old type of foot brace, which is still around, that consists of a bar running across the inside of the kayak from side to side. It can entrap feet, endangering the boater's life.

The Europeans have developed a new type of foot brace, which consists of a solid piece of plywood or plastic, cut to fit inside the kayak. The board, on which the feet are braced, prevents the situation in which the boat collides head on with a rock, knocking the kayaker off the foot peddles and forcing him farther in the boat. In severe cases, a kayaker can be jammed so tightly in his boat that he becomes entrapped. The board is spring loaded to absorb the shock from particularly bad collisions that could cause undue stress on the kayaker's ankles. Normally, this situation is not a major problem, but these braces are not a bad idea for those planning to run rocky, steeply dropping rivers.

Knee, Thigh, and Hip Braces. Various types of fiber glass, plastic, and foam knee, thigh, and hip bracing systems are incorporated into kayaks to provide the boater with a tight, secure fit. To paddle, roll, and run white water effectively, the anchoring system is essential. The tight fit transforms the boater's body motions to the boat. It is possible to add foam on existing kayaks to beef up the bracing system. Many kayakers now are cementing mini-cell foam or other types of foam to the sides of kayaks to conform to the hips and the outside of the thighs. Additional foam extends from the knee braces to the inside of the mid-thighs, creating an extensive bracing system and giving the boater superb control. The one caution with any bracing is to be sure you easily can come out of the boat if for some reason you need to.

Seat. The seat should be comfortable and snug. In some kayaks, different-sized seats are available. If they are not, you easily can make the seat more snug by cementing ethafoam or mini-cell foam to the sides of the boat near your hips, or by gluing closed-cell foam (the same type used in Ensolite sleeping pads) to the kayak seat.

Other Features. An important feature on all boats are grab loops on the bow and stern of the kayak, which are necessary for tying the kayak to cartop carriers or pulling a capsized boat ashore. Other features found on some kayaks include removable seats, back braces, and other specialties the particular manufacturer uses to spice up his boat.

Building a Kayak

Fiber glass is not a difficult medium to work with, and many kayakers have built their own boats. Boating clubs often have boat building

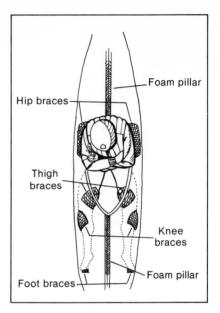

Bracing system

Grab loops are useful for tying kayaks to cartop carriers and pulling capsized boats to shore.

In building a kayak, several layers of precut cloth are placed into a waxed mold.

workshops and clinics, and it is possible to do it on your own if you can borrow or rent a mold.

First, precut cloth is placed in several layers on a waxed mold. Resin is mixed and brushed on, saturating the cloth. A deck and hull are formed in this manner in the mold, allowed to harden, and removed from the mold. Then the deck and hull are seamed together and the cockpit rim, seat, and foot braces are attached. The best book available for building kayaks and canoes is Charles Walbridge's *Boatbuilder's Manual*. For those wishing to delve deeper into boat building, *Advanced Fabrication Techniques for Whitewater Boats* also is available. See the "Sources" chapter for information about both books.

Buying a Kayak

Before making a purchase, check with kayaking friends. Try out different types of boats. How comfortable you feel and how well you are braced in a kayak determine how the boat will respond for you. For recreational white water, it is wise to stay away from the hot slalom racing designs or wild-water or downriver boats (see the "Kayak Design" section earlier in this chapter) and stick with white-water play-boats or white-water touring kayaks.

Buying a used boat is a good way of getting started in kayaking without a large investment. Check the rim. If it is broken, it can be repaired, but it will require additional work time. Push on the hull and deck and see if any cracks show up. The fiber glass should flex and pop back in place. Reg Lake of River Touring Equipment (Brisbane, California) suggests putting your head inside a boat and holding it up to the sun. Flaws, fractures, and patches will show up as shadows. Sit in the boat. Does it feel comfortable? You can make it more comfortable by adding foam padding, but it will save you a lot of extra work if the boat feels good from the beginning.

Kayak Paddles

A kayak paddle is built with a blade on each end, set at ninety degrees to each other. The paddle must be rotated as the kayaker makes a stroke on each side. This arrangement helps cut down air resistance when paddling into strong winds and water resistance when paddling through big waves.

Blades.   Kayak paddles also are constructed with flat or curved blades. Both blades have advocates. Flat blades are the same on each side and there is no confusion about which side is the power face of the blade when paddling or rolling. They are effective for back stroking and some boaters recommend them for beginners.

The most popular paddles for kayaking have curved blades, available in different types of curvature, and are powerful and good on technical rivers. Since the concave curve of the blade is the power face, this type can be confusing to a new paddler if he is disoriented underwater while getting ready for a roll, but with a little practice, most beginning paddlers can adapt easily. Curved-bladed paddles are manufactured with "left" or "right" control. As you turn the paddle shaft with each stroke, one of your hands consistently does the turning while the other allows the shaft to rotate. If you turn it with your right hand, you are a right-handed paddler and need to buy a right-grip paddle. Left-handed paddlers use a left-grip paddle. The two are not interchangeable, and it is important to know the difference if you buy a curved-bladed paddle. Tom Wilson of Phoenix Products (Tyner, Kentucky) suggests at the onset that beginners should learn to "control" or "grip" the paddle with the right handle since the right-grip paddle is easier to obtain. Other kayakers believe the control hand is something that develops naturally and whatever comes naturally is the way to go.

Wood or Synthetic.   Wood kayak paddles are preferred by some paddlers because the wood feels good and has a warm touch, but they also demand extra care. Fiber-reinforced paddles that are made from epoxies, Kevlar, and other tough synthetics and that have wrapped aluminum shafts are among the strongest of paddles and require little care. Using injected, molded plastic paddles is a way to cut costs, but some of these paddles have breakage problems and they often do not feel so comfortable as other paddles.

Shaft.   An important feature on any type of kayak paddle is an oval shaft. It provides a better grip than a round one and, by the feel, the paddler knows how the blade of the paddle is oriented as he makes strokes.

Length.   The size of the paddle generally is judged by the height of the kayaker. The "Sizing Paddles" chart illustrates one way that paddlers size their paddle for white water. Other paddlers say that 82 inches (208 centimeters) is standard size, with personal preference going 2 inches (5 centimeters) on either side. Ron Mattson feels that a shorter paddle can be used more effectively for accelerating to catch waves for surfing and playing. So there is a lot of leeway in your choice of paddle.

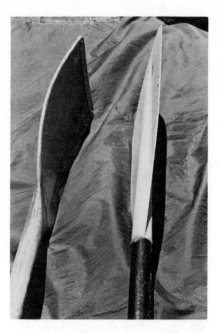

Curved blade paddle (*left*); flat blade paddle (*right*)

Spray Skirts

A spray skirt fits around the kayaker's waist and is attached to the rim of the cockpit by means of an elastic shock cord. The most common and most comfortable is made of neoprene, the same material used in wet suits, but nylon skirts also are available. Spray skirts come in kits, or can

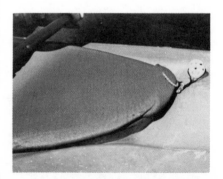

The shock cord or strap on the front of the spray skirt should be left on top. If the skirt binds, the strap can be pulled to release it.

Sizing Paddles

Height of Kayaker	Size of Paddle
Short (up to 5 feet 6 inches)	80 to 82 inches (204 to 208 centimeters)
Average (5 feet 6 inches to 6 feet 2 inches)	82 to 84 inches (208 to 214 centimeters)
Tall (6 feet 2 inches and over)	84 to 86 inches (214 to 220 centimeters)

be fairly easily made, with some sewing knowledge, from waterproof nylon material. All spray skirts should be designed with a strap or cord on the outside that can be pulled to detach the spray skirt from the rim if it does not pop off when the boater is forced to eject himself from the kayak. Jamming normally is not a problem, but with any spray skirt, try it out several times to be sure it releases without a hitch.

Helmets

Helmets are a must for kayaking. When a kayaker flips upside down, his head is exposed to rocks before he rolls. In addition, a kayaker swimming a rapid requires head protection. A friend of mine tipped upside down in a very shallow rapid in low-water conditions. From above, I watched his upside-down kayak jerk up and down as his helmet banged

Before getting under way, check to make sure the helmet is secure.

over boulders on the river bottom. He eventually got out of his kayak and stood up in water shallower than his knees. Because of his helmet, he did not have a bruise or scrape. Helmets also are worn as a safety precaution by some canoeists and rafters.

When choosing a helmet for white-water use, the following are some points to keep in mind:

- Choose a helmet that has a lining of crushable foam or closed-cell foam at least one-half-inch thick, with up to an inch providing even more protection.
- Many boaters advise against helmets with large holes in the shell, such as in the old-style hockey helmets once used for white water. Dick Held was on a trip where a stick penetrated one of the holes in the helmet of a kayaking companion, badly cutting him so that he needed stitches.
- The helmet should protect the forehead, temples, ears, and back of the head. Charles Walbridge, safety chairman of the American Canoe Association, explains that impact with river obstructions most likely will occur to the side of the head rather than directly to the top.
- The helmet should be comfortable and snug, and should not tend to come off the boater's head when he is doing rolls.

A cheap temporary alternative to buying a helmet is to use a motorcycle or football helmet. They are heavy, but relatively safe. Some boaters use rock climbing helmets, which are certainly better than the hockey-style helmets, but many climbing helmets leave the temple area exposed, and some have a tendency to roll off the back of the head, with the chin strap ending up around the neck of the boater.

Foam Pillars

Ethafoam—or better yet, mini-cell pillars—that keep the kayak deck from collapsing on a boater's legs should be used in any kayak, whether it is plastic or fiber glass. If you are adding pillars to your kayak, use full-length walls tightly jammed in the boat and supported by blocks of foam glued on either side of the pillars. If you do not glue the blocks in place, the presence of the foam walls may be a greater hazard than the one they are designed to prevent. The foam blocks keep the walls from rotating out of place and entrapping your legs.

Flotation Bags

A kayak needs flotation or it will sink. Various vinyl bags are available to provide flotation. One type, called a storage flotation bag, has an opening in which you stuff your gear for overnight or day trips. When sealed, the bag keeps the gear dry and provides flotation. Flotation bags with or without storage also are available for kayaks with foam walls.

The trouble with vinyl flotation bags is that they can be easily damaged. Use extreme care when using them. A new, strong nylon float bag by Voyageur's is now available that is more expensive but more rugged (see the "Equipment" section in the "Sources" chapter). I have known people who have constructed float bags out of light raft-patching material, which worked adequately.

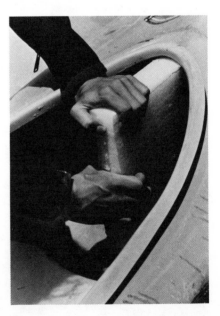

Putting a foam wall in place

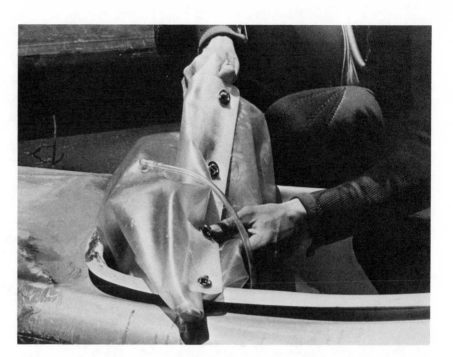

Overnight gear can be placed in the opening of a storage flotation bag. The bag is shoved in the boat and inflated to provide flotation for the kayak and to keep gear dry.

Break-down Paddles

On any kayak trip, it is a good idea to have one or more spare paddles available in your group. If you are not supported by rafts, it will be necessary to carry the spare paddle in the kayak. Special break-down paddles that detach in the middle are made for this purpose.

Other White-Water Craft

Open Canoes.　Increasing numbers of boaters, especially in the East, have been pushing the limits of canoeing to an extent never believed possible. Even the Colorado River has been run in open canoes. The new ABS/Royalex and polyethylene canoes are extremely durable, and can be popped back in shape if dented. Canoes for white water should have high enough sides to keep large amounts of water from splashing inside. Some canoeists recommend fifteen-inch sides for white water. The bottom of the boat should not have raised keel strips and needs some amount of rocker for good turning. The canoe should provide a bracing system so the canoeist can be secured in the boat, but also be able to escape easily if the boat capsizes. Thwarts or seats should not be placed so low as to trap his feet. Finally, a canoe for white-water use should have extra flotation. Some boaters use large blocks of foam placed in the middle of the canoe.

These are just a few suggestions. I will leave discussion of canoe techniques to those much more qualified than I. Two excellent sources on canoeing are *The Complete Wilderness Paddler* by James Davidson and John Rugge and the superbly illustrated *Path of the Paddle* by Bill Mason (see the "Books" section in the "Sources" chapter).

Folding Kayaks.　Folding kayaks were developed in Germany, where people needed a portable boat that could be packed in a bundle and carried with them on trains to the river.

Open canoe in white water

Single and double kayaks are available, with the single kayak being more suited to white water. People have pushed harder rapids in folding kayaks, but class II and III waters are, in most cases, the limit. Generally, these craft are more suited to easy rapids and flat water.

Inflatable Kayaks and Canoes.   The models with no decking, such as Tahitis, Piranahs, or Sea Eagles, surprisingly are very stable boats. They are, however, sluggish, poor at turning into eddies, and not nearly so maneuverable in rapids as a kayak or decked canoe.

The covered type of inflatable, looking much like a kayak, has an inflatable deck and hull. It handles much like a rigid kayak, but not quite so well. The decked inflatable has a fiber glass seat and cockpit rim, and the paddler uses a spray skirt. It can be rolled upright if it capsizes. This type of boat is useful for flying into short landing strips or gravel bars on remote wilderness rivers. It can be packed into a large rucksack for long portages around unrunnable white water, but it is very specialized and the most dangerous of white-water craft since if it is pinned against a rock, the deck can entrap the boater.

Sportyaks.   This small, 7- or 8-foot (2.0- to 2.5-meter) craft looks like a small plastic bathtub with oars. It is a fun little boat and has even been oared successfully down the Colorado River, but obviously it cannot carry much gear.

Sources of Kayaks and Other Equipment

The river runner has a wide choice of manufacturers and mail order suppliers. Any item described in this book is available from the companies listed in the "Sources" chapter.

Inflatable kayak

DAY AND OVERNIGHT EQUIPMENT

Bill March, an English friend, was along the first time I attempted to paddle a kayak on a river. He gave me instructions as I nodded and squeezed into the cramped kayak. Wide-eyed and white-knuckled, I shakily paddled the tippy craft into the current. In a proper English accent, Bill chatted about leaning and bracing and stoppers and rocks, but the only thing I could think about was keeping the boat right side up. The rapids just around the bend had me worried.

Bill was still chatting as we dropped into them. I rose up over the first wave and down the next. A wave hit me on the side and started tipping the boat, and I flailed the paddle like a duck flapping across the top of the water. I regained my balance and paddled successfully through the rest of the rapids.

I loved it. I loved the feeling of waves breaking across the bow, spraying my face and leaving me with tingling excitement. But in my confidence, the kayak suddenly spun, throwing me off-balance to the outside and flipping upside down. I did not even think about a roll. All I knew was that I wanted no part of being upside down in that confining craft and practically jumped out of the cockpit before the boat was fully over.

I bobbed down through the next set of rapids and Bill paddled up and said, "Hang onto my canoe youth," and pulled me off to the shore.

Capsizing is just one of the experiences that most people go through when they learn how to kayak. Though a little frightening at first, a swim in carefully chosen water is not bad. With the wrong equipment, however, a simple swim to shore can be dangerous. In cold water without a wet suit, a person can develop hypothermia at an alarming rate. Without a helmet, a kayaker's head is dangerously exposed to rocks. A life jacket is most important because it keeps a swimmer safely afloat. In this chapter, we will explore the equipment and clothing that make kayaking and rubber boating safe and comfortable. An extensive list of these items is provided in "Checklists" at the end of the book.

Life Jackets

People swim through rapids all the time without life jackets—some make it, some do not. Undertows, cold water, rocks, and turbulent currents all make it hard enough to swim, much less keep your head above water without the aid of a life jacket. In the seventies when interest in white water burgeoned, a rash of deaths occurred on the Chattooga River in the southeastern United States. In eight of the early deaths on the river, seven victims wore no life jackets and the eighth person had it draped over his shoulders. The Chattooga message could not have been clearer about whether a boater should wear a life jacket.

Types of Life Jackets. Different types of life jackets (often termed personal flotation devices or PFDs) are available. The United States Coast Guard has developed a system of classifying PFDs. However, in the brief descriptions that follow, you will notice that just because a life jacket is approved by the Coast Guard does not mean that it is suitable for river running. Nonetheless, since we are stuck with the system for awhile, it is important to understand it and then choose a life jacket that is adequate for white-water needs.

Type I life jacket, sometimes called a "Mae West"

The *type I* PFD has the greatest buoyancy (at least twenty-two pounds) of all jackets and will float most unconscious people to a vertical position. It provides the best protection in terms of keeping a boater's head above the surface of the water in big, forceful rapids. The life jacket is large, sometimes called a "Mae West" after the popular actress of Hollywood's glamorous thirties. Because of its shape, it feels uncomfortable to most boaters, who opt for the type III jackets. Some boaters claim that the buoyancy is too much, keeping a kayaker suspended too high in a hole and in some situations preventing him from washing out. The advantages and disadvantages of high flotation PFDs are argued by good boaters on both sides, and the final choice is up to the individual boater. One thing is certain: high flotation life jackets will ride a swimming boater higher and keep his head above turbulent water longer than any other type and that is of primary concern to most recreational boaters. Recently some high flotation, type III life jackets have appeared on the market offering nearly all the advantages of type I.

Type II PFDs also turn an unconscious swimmer to a vertical position, but they are slower and the buoyancy (for adults a minimum of 15½ pounds) is less than in type I. A common life jacket in this category is the so-called "horse collar," which is rectangular with a lengthwise split. The split ends at a hole at the top for the head. In turbulent water, this type of jacket has slipped off some people. The jacket is suitable for boating in lakes, but *completely inadequate for white water*.

The type II life jacket is unsuitable for white-water use.

The *type III* PFD is the most commonly used life jacket for a variety of water sports. It will not upright an unconscious person, but it will keep a conscious person in a vertical or near vertical position. The minimum buoyancy requirement for type III jackets is 15½ pounds, less than that for type I. It looks like a jacket completely encircling the wearer, usually with a zipper and additional ties for added security. The variety of styles and sizes available makes this type of PFD very comfortable and by far the most popular choice for white-water kayakers and many rafters.

A new style of type III PFD exceeds the minimum buoyancy requirements for type I with as much as almost thirty pounds of flotation, yet offers all the comfort advantages of type IIIs. Boaters who feel safer with high flotation now have a comfortable option within the type III

Most kayakers use the type III life jacket.

This style of the type V life jacket was designed for rafters.

category. Kayakers might be interested to note that as a side benefit, a high buoyancy life jacket will hold him high in the water on the rolling side, which makes the roll easier, after a boat capsizes.

Type IV is the seat cushion and ring buoy category, which has no application for white water.

The *type V* category has several different types of jackets, one of which is approved for commercial white-water use. It has the same minimum buoyancy requirement (twenty-two pounds) as type I, but it will not turn an unconscious person to a vertical position. It rapidly has become the most popular life jacket for rafters, and rightly so since it was designed for rafting. An occasional kayaker may use one, but the type V design is more suited for the oaring or paddling of a raft.

Choice, Fit, and Materials. The choice, then, for kayaking is type III and for rafting type V, with a few rafters and kayakers still preferring the large type Is. In addition to choosing the correct type, it is important to have a good fit, from both a comfort and safety standpoint. Choose a life jacket that fits snugly and comfortably. Wave your arms around in an exaggerated paddling or oaring motion. The jacket should not bind or abrade bare skin. Stay away from the stiff and uncomfortable vinyl-dipped life jackets in the type III category, which are used by water-skiers. Many boaters prefer type III life jackets constructed with the narrow baffles (each baffle approximately 1 ½ to 2 inches wide) since the small baffling tends to conform better to the body. You will find that some PFDs, whether they are a type III or V, are made from a soft fill material. Though jackets with the softer fill generally cost a little more than stiffer jackets, boaters also will appreciate the added comfort.

Kayakers should double-check that a life jacket fits properly while sitting in a kayak with a spray skirt on. Some life jackets should be avoided by kayakers as they are cut so long that the spray skirt barely can be put in place.

Life jackets are filled with different substances. You still will find some type Is filled with kapok, a natural fiber. Kapok is encased in plastic baffles, which can and do break, allowing water to seep in and destroy the buoyancy of the jacket. If you have a kapok jacket, treat it like a baby. It is, however, a filling of the past. A variety of reliable types of closed-cell foams now provides flotation for PFDs.

Some life jackets come with a convenient pocket, in which you can carry a knife, fire starter, matches, and other items. If you do not have one on your present PFD, it is not too difficult to sew one on.

Clothing for Dry Boats

The type of clothing you use for white-water trips will be determined by two situations: riding in a fairly dry inflatable raft or dory, or riding in a fairly wet boat with lots of water splashing. (The latter situation is described in the next section.)

Warm Days and Chilly Days. On warm, sunny days in summer the common attire is shorts, a T-shirt, tennis shoes, and a hat for protection from the sun. No matter how warm the weather is, however, any river can get chilly if clouds mask the sun and the wind comes up. If that happens, you will want to have extra clothing along. A nylon wind parka and nylon wind or rain pants worn over the T-shirt and shorts may suffice. For more warmth, wool shirts, wool sweaters, and wool pants are good since even if the wool gets wet, it still retains some of its insulating qualities. When it is cool avoid cotton clothing such as jeans. Cotton has no insulating ability when it gets wet, and on rainy, cool days, wearing jeans and a cotton shirt quickly can chill your body and lead to hypothermia.

A synthetic replacement for wool is fiberpile or simply pile. It is a fluffy type of material that feels cozy and comfortable against the skin. Its advantages are its light weight and its ability to dry quickly. On one cold day on a river, I dropped my fiberpile sweater in water sloshing in the bottom of the boat. It was sopping wet, but I wrung it out and shook it vigorously to rid it of additional water. It immediately was comfortable enough to wear and kept me warm the rest of the day. Many different styles are available at outdoor shops. Fiberpile material also is available at fabric shops, and a shirt, sweater, or jacket can be sewn inexpensively by a seamstress. *However, pile alone, without wind protection, is inadequate.* Since wind can blow easily through pile, it is necessary to carry a Windbreaker or nylon jacket of some type to cover the pile.

Fiberpile jackets and other pile clothing are warm on and off the river and are an excellent synthetic replacement for wool.

If the weather is colder, you may want to wear long underwear under your clothing. Wool is good, but an excellent synthetic underwear is polypropylene. It has tremendous ability to transfer moisture away from the skin, keeping you warmer than other materials. I have used it extensively on month-long winter trips and found it to be some of the warmest, most comfortable underwear available.

Rain Gear. Rain gear is essential on any river trip. If it gets a little cool, sometimes just slipping on a rain jacket will be enough to keep you warm. Or you may slip on rain pants over your shorts to protect your legs. The rain jacket and separate rain pants are the best system for river running. Ponchos are not a good choice since the long tails of material get in the way when loading, unloading, and rowing, and are particularly dangerous, restricting swimming, if the boat flips over.

The best materials for rain gear are waterproof nylon, which is lightweight, or the thicker rubberized nylon, sometimes called "slickers," which is heavier. You must seal the seams on rain gear if the manufacturer has not done so. Seam sealer can be purchased from outdoor stores and applied easily at home. Do not forget to seal the seams or else water will seep through on rainy days and wet your clothing underneath. Manufacturers of good rain gear minimize the seams in the shoulder area since this is a primary place for water to seep through.

From my experiences, rain gear made of old or new generation Gore-Tex and material like it do not stand up under long and heavy use, and for true rain protection it is best to stick with fabrics you know will work.

Wear your life jacket over a rain parka. If you ever have to swim, the life jacket will prevent the rain parka from floating up and restricting your motions.

Feet. Tennis shoes with or without wool socks are commonly worn by river runners. Feet get wet from climbing in and out of the boat or from sitting in water on the floor of the boat. For comfort many boaters wear wet suit bootees inside the tennis shoes, which they buy a size or two larger to fit over the bootee. Some ultrathin bootees are available that do not require wearing larger-sized shoes. Wet suit bootees are not too expensive and can be purchased from catalog outfits, outdoor shops, skin diving stores, or well-stocked white-water shops. Some bootees are available with a hard bottom so you can walk around, but usually the tennis shoe–bootee arrangement gives you more support for scouting

Some boaters wear wet suit bootees inside large-sized tennis shoes to keep their feet warm on the river.

Pogies allow a kayaker's hands to stay warm while he grips the paddle with his bare hands.

Paddling jacket under a type III life jacket

Farmer John wet suit

rapids, climbing over boulders, and hiking. Since river shoes are wet most of the day, they tend to fall apart after a season or two of use. Rather than sink a lot of money into a good pair of tennis shoes, many boaters buy a cheap pair at a discount store and replace them every couple of years. Some boaters recommend a special type of shoe for rivers, which is available from white-water suppliers.

Hands. Many oarsmen use leather gloves to prevent blisters. As the weather becomes colder some use Pogies, which originally were created for kayakers, over the oar. Pogies, designed by a world-class racer named Bonnie Losick, are a covering that fits around the shaft of the paddle or handle of the oar and allows your bare hand to grip the handle directly for good control and also keeps your hand warmer than if you were using a bare handle.

Head. In sunny weather boaters use a variety of hats—from cowboy hats to baseball caps, from visors to felt hats. Most of the body's heat is lost through the head and neck, and it is important to keep this area insulated in cold weather. One of the best hats is a wool stocking cap. For cooler weather, a wool hat called a balaclava, which pulls down to cover the neck area yet leaves a face opening, is very warm.

Clothing for Wet Boats

"Wet boats" include kayaks, decked canoes, paddle rafts, wet oar rafts, and small inflatables.

Hot Days. On hot days, you will be able to get by with a swimsuit or shorts, and perhaps a light nylon Windbreaker or paddling jacket. A paddling jacket is simply a beefed-up nylon Windbreaker, usually made of thicker nylon material and often constructed with neoprene cuffs and collars. It helps to keep wind off the upper body and thus is warm. The other suggestions for warm weather clothing in the preceding "Clothing for Dry Boats" section apply as well.

Wet Suits. More often than not, the river water will be cold, and paddling on rivers, even when the sun is shining, can be chilly once you get wet. In a kayak, paddle raft, or small inflatable, there is no way of keeping dry. When you are getting wet, the best system for staying warm is a wet suit. Various types of suits are available, including pants, long-sleeved jackets, short-sleeved jackets, sleeveless jackets, and so on.

Many kayakers prefer the sleeveless farmer John style with full length or short length legs. Also popular among surfers, this wet suit provides protection to the legs and most of the upper body. I wear my farmer John with long legs even when the temperature is above ninety degrees Fahrenheit, but I am the type of person who gets cold easily so I do not mind the extra insulation when it is hot. If the temperature drops, you can add a paddling jacket or Windbreaker. Or what an increasing number of kayakers and rafters do is add a pile sweater and/or pile pants (see the "Clothing for Dry Boats" section) plus a paddling jacket. The pile retains warmth when wet, does not restrict motions, and dries quickly. Reg Lake of River Touring Equipment (Brisbane, California) warns that "a wet suit should be worn anytime the water is cold and there is a good chance of being immersed. Wool or pile and a paddling jacket are great for deflecting a splash and retaining body heat after being immersed, but a wet suit is your only protection while immersed." If the weather and water are colder still, you can slip on a wet suit jacket. By beginning with the farmer John, you have a versatile system that can be used on warm days or chilly, rainy days just by adding a paddling jacket, pile sweater, or wet suit jacket.

For whatever wet suit system you use, the best thickness of material is the ⅛-inch (0.3-centimeter) size, which allows the wet suit to stretch more than thicker material does, making it easier to paddle. A wet suit for paddling should fit looser than one you might use for skin diving. It should not be overly loose, but should fit comfortably, with some extra room in the arms and legs.

A wet suit with a nylon-lined interior is stronger and easier to get in and out of than other suits. Nylon lining on the outside, however, makes the suit stiffer and harder to paddle. Ron Mattson of Cascade Outfitters (Monroe, Oregon) adds that the nylon exterior holds water, and wind blowing over the wet nylon will cause a small but additional chilling effect.

When it gets cold, you can add wool or polypropylene underwear under the wet suit to increase its warmth. If you indulge in winter boating, try thicker wet suit jackets worn with wool or pile underneath and a paddling jacket over everything. Wet suit hoods are available for the head. For the feet, wear tennis shoes over wet suit bootees.

Hands.   There is nothing more uncomfortable than paddling with cold hands, and keeping the hands warm in cool or cold weather can make the difference between fun and misery. Pogies, as explained previously, allow your hands to grip the paddle shaft directly. Inner liners of pile also are available to increase warmth. A few boaters swear by thick rubber gloves. Nylon mittens with a rough material on the palm are used by some boaters, and for further warmth, wool or pile mittens can be worn underneath. Other boaters use thin, wet suit mittens (with no nylon layer on the outside), which work well in frigid water.

Day Equipment for Rafting

The suggestions made in "Checklists" at the end of this book will help you decide what specific items to take on a day (or multi-day) trip. Let's single out a few of those items.

A repair kit is a must. At home, try to think of anything that can go wrong with your equipment and carry the tools and repair items needed to fix it. Inflatable rafts can be damaged, so you need to carry patch material, glue, and solvent that is recommended by the boat manufacturer as being compatible with your boat's material. For oar-powered boats, include extra oarlocks and extra screws, bolts, and nuts for the frame.

One of the most important items in a repair kit is duct tape. It has multiple uses. Eight years ago on a river trip, our party came across an old broken McKenzie boat that had been left abandoned for several years alongside a river. Using duct tape, we patched broken boards and sealed the many holes. When we were finished, the wood was barely visible under layers of tape. I borrowed a couple of spare oars, put my kayak inside, and ran the decrepit derelict the remainder of the week-long trip. We eventually got it off the river, though it was so badly damaged it never saw another river trip.

A first aid kit should be carried for any injuries that occur and sun screen lotions and sunglasses are important for protecting your skin and eyes from the sun's glare. (Rivers claim many sunglasses; the best

Rafters, especially with oar frames, should carry enough tools and parts to fix anything that goes wrong.

Protection from the sun's glare is essential on a river.

method of keeping yours from drowning is to tie them on your head with nylon cord or use an elastic strap.) Extra clothing is necessary for remaining warm and comfortable if the weather turns cold. Besides a knife, you will want matches carried in a waterproof container and a fire starter of some type. Fire starter can be solid fuel pellets, a candle, or other flammable substances that are so necessary to start a fire when the wood and tinder are soaked. It is a good idea for each boater to carry the knife, matches, and fire starter in his clothing or in a small pocket that has been sewn on the life jacket. Carry some extra food along even if you do not plan to have lunch on the river. On cold days, keep munching quick-energy food to provide energy and ward off hypothermia.

You will want a throw-rope rescue bag (a specially made bag with a throw line), cord or straps for lashing gear off the floor, a bow and a stern line of three-eighths-inch polypropylene, a pump, a water container, and perhaps a camera. You also will need a bucket (Bob Blackadar, an experienced rafter from Salmon, Idaho, recommends the five-gallon size) for bailing water out of the boat. A small bailer can be made by cutting the bottom out of a plastic bleach bottle that has a handle. If you do not have a bailer, rummage in the garbage cans at laundries, a gold mine for plastic bleach bottles.

Day Equipment for Kayaking

In addition to the kayak, paddle, flotation bags, helmet, spray skirt, and wet suit, you also will want a repair kit. Repair kits for day kayaking usually consist of one item — duct tape. It can repair most boat breakage well enough for you to get off the river. The more expensive type of duct tape is better in the long run since it does not delaminate, as the cheaper brands do.

Be sure to patch holes in the kayak before leaving on a trip. I went on one trip without fixing a number of bad leaks in my kayak. So much water leaked into my boat that, having nothing else, I used a plastic measuring cup as a bailer. After I was swallowed by several monstrous holes with a boat full of water, I decided that when a boater has to resort to using a measuring cup as a bailer, it is time to repair the boat.

You also will want to carry a first aid kit, matches and fire starter, a knife, some food, sunglasses, a paddling jacket, and a throw-rope rescue bag. A sponge is handy for removing water.

Gear for day trips can be stored in a small, waterproof, day storage bag, available at kayak shops. A friend of mine made a day bag by cutting a round cylinder of rubber off a truck inner tube. He sealed both ends with plastic closures that commonly are used for waterproof storage bags. The day bag can be clipped in behind the seat, but make the cord very short. Any cord in which a foot or hand can become entangled is dangerous.

Overnight Equipment

When you go on overnight or multi-day trips, you will want to be even more careful that the equipment you carry will make you as self-sufficient as possible. Repair kits should be extensive. Besides the equipment previously discussed under day equipment, you will want to take two pairs of shoes: one to use during the day and a dry pair to change into in the evening. For clothing in camp, it is nice to have a dry set to change into, if you can carry the extra weight. Otherwise, if you are going very light, use fiberpile clothing, a multi-use clothing that can be used during the day, yet dries rapidly enough to be used in camp at night. Other multi-use items of clothing are Gore-Tex and Klimate rain pants or regular nylon wind pants, which can be pulled over a pair of shorts to make adequate and comfortable evening wear. You will need various other small items suggested in "Checklists" at the end of the book. I will use the remainder of the chapter to discuss larger items, such as tarps, tents, sleeping bags, environmental equipment, as well as cameras.

Tarps. Various types of lightweight nylon tarps are available from outdoor stores for use on river trips. Erected in any number of ways, tarps can be tied to trees, bushes, oars, or paddles creating a lean-to, or the four corners of the tarp can be staked out and a stick placed under the middle to make a pyramid shape. Tarps also can be used to provide protection in the cooking and kitchen area. The advantage of nylon tarps is that they are the lightest form of shelter and are useful for boaters trying to save weight and bulk.

Tarps are easy to make. It is just a matter of sewing nylon material together, adding loops of webbing at the corners and the sides for tie-down places, and sealing the seams.

With a tarp you also will need a ground cloth, which can consist of a sheet of plastic or a smaller waterproof tarp to fit under your sleeping bag.

The disadvantage of tarps is that they do not keep out mosquitoes. When my partner, Ike Gayfield, and I first started Mountain Folk, our mountain shop, we manufactured some equipment. One item Ike designed was a tarp with a width of mosquito netting sewed around the base. I have used the tarp for years in a number of places where the mosquitoes were thick, and it worked great. If you have a tarp, sew mosquito netting around its edge. When you set it up, stake out the four corners and use a stick as a center pole. In this way the bottom edge of the tarp is an equal distance above the ground, and with the mosquito netting touching the ground, the rascals are prevented from getting inside.

Try to find a protected spot to pitch your tarp when the weather looks threatening. I once set up a tarp on a sandy beach on a desert river in the

Tying tent cords to rocks rather than to stakes works well when setting up a tent on a sandy beach.

southwestern United States. A wind came up during the night and blew through the tarp for several hours, sand and grit seeping into our sleeping bags the entire time. We tossed and scraped against the sand in our bags for a few hours, then the rain started. It blew through the tarp, turning our shelter for the evening into a mess of soggy, muddy sleeping bags. The next night, having learned, I set up the tarp behind a screen of bushes.

Tents.   Tents come in many different styles and colors. Most of them are constructed of lightweight nylon materials, though there are a few heavy, canvaslike models available. The dome- and tunnel-shaped tents are the most efficient as far as use of space is concerned. But tunnel and dome tents usually are more expensive than the A- or pyramid-shaped styles.

No-see-um netting, a fine mesh that keeps out the smallest and peskiest of critters, is available on many tents. Various Gore-Tex tents and tents made of similar waterproof, breathable materials are available, which some people rave about, but traditional backpacking tents are cheaper and do just as good a job.

The standard tent system for keeping out rain has a breathable tent interior and a waterproof tent fly placed over the top of the tent. Completely waterproof tents are available, but to get a good one that works well, you will have to put more money into it.

Sleeping Bags.   Basically, two types are available: the synthetic fiberfills such as PolarGuard, Thinsulate, and so on; and down. The advantage of the fiberfills is that they absorb very little water, and even if they become wet, they still provide some warmth for the sleeper. In most cases, fiberfill bags are a good choice for river runners.

Though fiberfill bags are fairly light, they still are not so light nor do they pack down into as small a stuff bag as down bags. On trips where you must cut down on bulk and shave off ounces, such as on a self-contained kayak trip, you may want to use a down bag. When down becomes wet, however, it is worthless as an insulator and takes a long time to dry. You must be absolutely sure it will not get wet. Double sealing a down bag in waterproof bags before packing it on a trip is not a bad idea.

The mummy-shaped bag is the warmest and lightest style of bag, but for sleepers who must have room, rectangular-shaped bags also are available. Boaters who like to snuggle up with their sweethearts can purchase zip-together models.

Sleeping Pads.   A sleeping pad of some type is necessary insulation under the sleeping bag. Various pads are available, such as Ensolite, blue cell foam, or polyurethane foam with a nylon cover. All of these are available at outdoor stores.

Some people prefer air mattresses. For cold trips, however, stick to the various types of foam pads. They are warmer.

Equipment to Minimize Environmental Impact.   Before leaving on a multi-day float trip, you should plan to bring equipment that helps minimize your group's impact on the environment. This aspect of river camping will be discussed more thoroughly in the chapter about camping, but let's consider a few items. All litter and garbage should be carried out from the river. If a lot of garbage is carried, such as on a raft trip, the plastic bag holding the garbage can be reinforced with a burlap sack or nylon stuff bag.

Human waste is a major problem on heavily used rivers, and governmental agencies managing the river may require portable toilets. Various portable toilets are available at camper and trailer supply stores.

A reliable portable toilet can be made from a toilet seat, two heavy-duty garbage bags, and a large ammo can called a rocket box, measuring the equivalent of 11 by 12 by 5½ inches.

If a stove is used, you eliminate the need to build fires and consume wood, which is becoming rare on some rivers. If you do use a fire, then you should use some type of fire pan to contain the ashes. Fire pans are available from river supply houses, or you can have a welder make one for you. For ease of packing, it can be constructed so it fits in one of the boat boxes on your boat or large enough so it fits under a cooler. To keep ashes from spilling, the sides of the fire pan should be at least five inches high. A grill can be placed over it for ease of cooking.

Kayakers also should develop methods that minimize environmental impact. A hub cap easily can be stored in a kayak to serve as a fire pan for small fires with cooking done easily and quickly on a small fire using small-diameter sticks. When overnighting on rivers where fires are environmentally unacceptable, small backpacking stoves can be carried. Backpacking stoves are convenient and in cold, hypothermic weather conditions, provide hot drinks and food immediately.

Cooking Gear.   If you are traveling light, all you need is a pot or two, a stove, and fuel. For eating utensils, a spoon and a plastic cup work fine and take up little room.

For luxurious trips, you may decide to use the traditional Dutch oven for preparing fine outdoor cuisine (see the "Dutch Oven Cookery" section in the "River Cuisine" chapter). Most river runners use cast-iron Dutch ovens, though some use lighter weight aluminum Dutch ovens with satisfaction. You also can carry large pots for soups, a coffee pot for hot drinks, and a frying pan, if desired. Fresh foods must be carried in sturdy coolers. Several good, plastic coolers are available. (Gott-brand coolers are particularly rugged and able to withstand the abuse of river trips.)

Water

Unfortunately, most river water is unfit to drink. Even wilderness rivers may be infected with bugs such as *Giardia* that cause intestinal problems. Whether you bring water from home or purify river water, you will need water containers. Various containers are available on the market, but plastic milk or bleach bottles work just as well.

Safety and Rescue Equipment

Life jackets, of course, are essential, as is a good first aid kit. A throw-rope rescue bag also should be readily available in every raft or kayak on a trip. By far the best ropes are those that are specially made to fit in a stuff bag (see the chapter about safety). In addition, some rafters carry a winch to use in rescuing pinned boats. A signal mirror can be useful in flagging down an aircraft in emergencies. Some boaters are equipped with radios, but I once carried a powerful radio into a remote area and made contact only once on the twenty-three-day trip. Radios can be helpful, but they have their limitations, and it is wise to consider the pros and cons if you ever feel you need one.

When fires are permitted, fire pans should be used to minimize impact on the campsites.

Cameras

Part of the fun of a river trip is recording it for remembrance at a later time. Some people take along waterproof cameras such as the under-water Nikonos. An underwater camera is particularly useful for kayakers or C-1 boaters, who sit low and constantly are getting wet. Various camera hitches for underwater cameras used by boaters are available at camera and outdoor shops. To prevent the camera from swinging up and hitting you in the face when you are not using it, get a hitch that can hold the camera securely against your chest.

Waterproof housings are available for cameras, and boaters particu-larly may be interested in a flexible waterproof housing. This housing, adaptable to most cameras and lenses, is constructed with a window for the camera lens and a built-in glove for focusing and making exposure and aperture changes. The flexible camera housing is reasonably priced, available at camera supply shops, and a good choice for boaters who cannot afford to add an underwater camera to their existing camera gear. Small waterproof vinyl- or nylon-coated bags can be purchased for carrying cameras. Also available is a protective type of camera bag that blows up, forming a cushion of air around the camera.

Rigid plastic containers are available for carrying cameras in rafts and larger craft. The most common container for this purpose, how-ever, is the metal ammo can. Although heavy, it is less expensive than plastic, and padding placed inside provides an extra measure of protec-tion for the camera.

Thoroughly test any waterproof container you use for your camera. Fill the container with water and be sure nothing leaks through seams and, in particular, through the closure.

Final Check

Before embarking on a day, overnight, or multi-day trip, check through your checklist (see "Checklists" at the end of the book) to be sure you have everything. With the large amount of equipment involved on river trips, especially if you choose the luxurious style, it is easy to forget something.

Double-check your equipment. Be sure everything is in working order. Does the stove work? Do the oars fit in the oarlocks? Does the kayak have any holes? At the put-in point of one river trip, we started blowing up the boats and found nine holes in one raft and ten holes in the other. We spent most of our first day gluing patches on the boats and were delayed so long by repairs that we barely ran three miles of the river before dark. If boats and equipment are fixed at home, the trip at least will start off well.

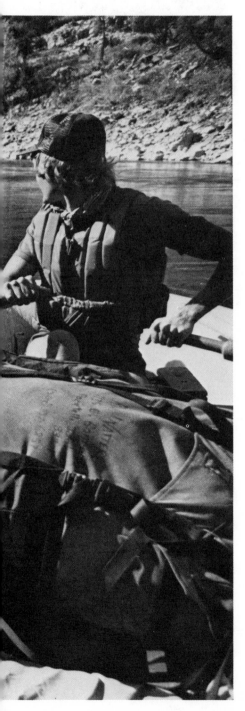

DOWN THE RIVER

Preparing for the last river trip this summer was hectic. Unrolling my rubber boat, I found several holes that I had forgotten to repair, and I reluctantly spent two extra, unplanned hours cutting and gluing on patches. Food and supplies for the week trip were heaped on tables and strewed across the floor. Three or four members of our frazzled party made several unsuccessful attempts to pack the huge pile of food in the few containers we had, while I ran off searching in stores across town for odds and ends of missing items necessary for the trip.

Eventually, five-gallon plastic buckets, used to hold mayonnaise, were acquired from a food service operation and, much to the relief of those in charge of food, solved the food storage problem. All the last-minute items were bought. We stuffed coolers in the van for seats and filled the pickup truck with rubber boats, waterproof bags, and food containers. On the trailer behind the pickup, we lashed frames, oars, paddles, and life jackets wherever space was available. Two kayaks were strapped on last, nearly hidden by helmets, ropes, pots, and bailing buckets dangling from cords. At last, we accomplished the seemingly impossible task of getting out of town. Relaxing as we drove down the highway, we joked about how next time we would be better organized.

The last of the long drive to the river was down a descending, bumpy road. The kayaks swayed, and buckets banged and clanged against the trailer. Finally reaching the river, we stiffly trotted to the river's edge, glad to be free of the cramped vehicles.

Watching the river tumbling between boulders and disappearing around the corner, I felt a familiar pretrip nervousness. Mostly, however, I felt good to be back at the river. I felt good breathing pine-scented river air, standing with the upstream breeze lightly blowing against my face, feeling the enchantment, once again, of the never-ending flow of a river. I was excited and anxious to get under way and back on the river again.

The Put-In and Take-Out

Try to choose places to begin the trip that are slow enough for you to get the boats loaded without being swept down the river. Be sure you know the exact location of the take-out point. In some cases the take-out may not be obvious from the river. Memorize land features and leave some kind of marking, such as a ribbon tied to a tree, to help you locate it.

Rigging a Raft

Before putting in, everything must be lashed to the raft so no gear is sitting on the floor. If you are utilizing a boat without a frame, use the various D rings and other tie-on points on the boat for suspending your gear.

Tightly secure frames to D rings on the boat for a positive attachment. Avoid using nylon parachute cord to hold the frame. The pressures exerted by the water on the frame can easily break smaller-diameter cords. Thick nylon rope, nylon webbing, or wide straps are best.

On either frame or frameless boats, securely lash gear so that it not only will be held tightly in place if the craft flips, but also will be easy to put on and take off. One way to speed up the process is to use straps with buckles to avoid tying knots. Straps can be purchased or easily made out of webbing and buckles, which are available at horse supply, canvas, and outdoor shops. Gear bags with strong handles can be clipped directly to the frame or boat by using carabiners. Carabiners or other types of clips save time and are a welcome convenience.

If you do not have carabiners, clips, or straps, then rope will suffice. Bring along plenty since lashing rope is always in demand on river trips. When tying on gear, put your foot against the side of the boat, and pull hard on the rope before knotting it so that the lashing is snug. Tie knots that are easy to undo, yet strong.

When you have finished lashing down the gear, be sure no loose lines are left hanging. Loose lines have the dangerous tendency to wrap around legs. Tuck them in or cut off the excess.

Some boaters tie in the bailing bucket while others do not. If you tie in the bailer, use a short cord of three to four inches, so there is no chance of its wrapping around legs. Since the bailer is used often, the most convenient system is to attach a clip to the bailer, making it easy to clip it on and off when needed.

To save unnecessary work, assemble the boat and tie on gear as near to the river as possible.

Distribution of Weight in a Raft. Ideally, the load on an inflatable raft should be distributed so that the boat can turn or pivot quickly in preparation for a move in a rapid. This balance is achieved by placing most of the weight low and in the center of the boat. You already may have designed this concept into your frame (or the frame you purchased may have it) with boat boxes, coolers, or a gear suspension net in the middle of the boat. If not, tie most of the gear in the middle of the boat and leave the ends of the boat as light as possible. If you tie gear onto the ends, tie lighter items there and save heavier items for closer to the middle. Often when you must carry a lot of gear, you may not be able to achieve ideal weight distribution, but the idea is to pack as much as possible with this in mind.

Also, remember as you tie on gear to figure in the weight of paddlers or passengers and where you plan to have them sit. Though most weight should be toward the middle, some boaters like to place passengers and/or gear in the front, making it slightly heavier than the rear. A heavier bow helps prevent the boat from tending to spin around in the current when pointed downstream.

Other things to consider as you lash gear include:
- Certain items should be tied on last so that you can get at them

Rigging an oar raft

Strong wide straps (or thick rope) are used to tie frames to rafts.

quickly. Leave the day's lunch and/or snacks at the top so you will not have to dig through all the food containers to get to it. The first aid kit, rescue rope, camera, guidebook or map, and emergency kit (knife, matches, and fire starter) all should be easily accessible.

● Allow room for rowing. On oar boats, be sure no gear prevents the oarsman from moving his oars fully backward and forward. On one trip, I had a large pile of gear on a suspended net of webbing in the middle of my boat. My oar caught on a rock as the boat lunged forward. The oar handle hurtled against the pile of gear, holding the oar solid and straining it beyond its breaking point. With a loud bang, the oar snapped in two.

● The very last pieces of gear to go on an inflatable raft are the spare oars or paddles. Some boaters bring one spare, but two are an especially good safety measure on rocky, oar-battering rivers. With synthetic oars, both a fully assembled oar and one or two replacement blades should be carried along. Place the oars so that the oarsman easily and quickly can pick up the spare and slip it into the oarlock. Oars most often are broken in rapids, and the boatman must have the oar immediately available. The less time it takes to get the oar in place, the better. Most boaters simply place one of the spare oars on top of gear alongside the boat, not tying it in so it is ready to be snatched up when needed. The spare oar is usually the only item of equipment not secured.

The spare oar is kept untied and handy for times when it is needed right away.

Packing a Kayak

On a self-contained kayak trip, you need to pack everything in your boat. Special storage flotation bags are available to hold gear. As with rafts, as much weight as possible should be placed toward the middle of the boat to achieve the most efficient maneuverability. Because of the small amount of storage available, the heaviest items should be placed in the rear storage bag as close to the seat as possible, while the lightest items should be placed in the farthest ends of the storage bags.

Storing gear in kayaks with foam walls can be accomplished by using special split flotation bags. A solution used by some kayakers is to use a short foam wall that starts at the foot braces and extends to the front of the cockpit rim. Full foam walls from the bow to the cockpit rim are safest, so use this system only when the gear is so bulky that it is absolutely necessary. A regular storage flotation bag filled with gear then can be placed forward of the foam wall in the bow. In the stern of the kayak, a regular storage flotation bag can be used, or some people use a short rear wall just behind the seat and carry a full-sized storage bag behind the wall.

Floating as a Group

When floating as a group, whether your party consists of kayaks, inflatable rafts, or other craft, there are some things you must keep in mind.

Positioning.   Once on the river most boaters run their boats in a predetermined order. The most experienced boaters in the group run first and last, with the less experienced boaters in between. In this system, the lead boat is never passed, and the last boat (often called the sweep boat) never passes any boat. Each boat keeps the one behind in sight. Progess is made in spurts. The leader runs a set of rapids, then waits in an eddy below, allowing the others to catch up. If everyone is fine, he continues on. In this way everyone is accounted for, and if problems occur, all boaters are there, ready to help.

This system is accepted by most boaters as the safest way to float a river. Each boater keeps track of the others, and an experienced boater is available in the front and in the rear to help if someone has problems.

A group of experienced boaters who have about equal ability will use

Although experienced boaters are flexible in their approach to running in a group, a safe procedure among mixed groups is to run an experienced boater in the front and another at the rear of the group.

a more flexible system, with boats changing position and leads. Safe distances are maintained between boats, and as always, everyone keeps track of each other.

Distance between Boats.   The safe distance between boats differs depending on the situation. If you are following a boat, you will want to stay close enough so you can see how the boatman is running the rapid yet far enough away so that if the leader gets in trouble (broached on a rock or caught in a hole, for example) you will have time to find a place where you can stop. In order to give the boat in front plenty of room while on a winding stretch, you sometimes may not be able to maintain a position where you always can see the boat ahead. If for some reason you are doubtful about what is coming up, stop and take a look.

The second boater is not giving the one ahead enough room.

The lead boater can help others through by signaling the best route.

Waiting at the Bottom.   After a rapid of consequence, the lead boatman should pull off, waiting to be sure everyone makes it through. If something happens, the boater at the bottom of the rapid is available to help. From the bottom, he may be able to point out the best route to others who are just entering the rapid.

Signals.   Be sure to talk about what signals you will use on the river. Keep them simple. The standard signals adapted by the American Whitewater Affiliation (you can write to them for a copy of their signals and safety code at the address noted in the "Periodicals" section in the "Sources" chapter; see the river signals illustrations for the visual signals) in their words include:

STOP—Potential hazard ahead. Wait for "all clear" signal before proceeding, or scout ahead. Form a horizontal bar with your paddle or outstretched arms. Move up and down to attract attention, using a pumping motion with paddle or flying motion with arms. Those seeing the signal should pass it back to others in the party.
HELP/EMERGENCY—Assist the signaler as quickly as possible. Give three long blasts on a police whistle while waving a paddle, helmet or life vest [or oar] over your head in a circular motion. If a whistle is not available, use the visual signal alone. A whistle is best carried on a lanyard attached to the shoulder of a life vest.

ALL CLEAR—Come ahead (in the absence of other directions, proceed down the center). Form a vertical bar with your paddle or one arm held high above your head. Paddle blade should be turned flat for maximum visibility. To signal direction or a preferred course through a rapid around obstruction, lower the previously vertical "all clear" by 45 degrees toward the side of the river with the preferred route. Never point toward the obstacle you wish to avoid.

A.

Be clear at the beginning what signals mean what. A friend of mine paddled around a corner on a river in high water to find himself in the big, grinding waves of a chaotic rapid. He looked at his friends waiting at the bottom of the rapid and saw a scene of frantic waving. Some pointed to the right, some pointed to the left, and others flailed their arms. He went down the middle and dropped over a huge hole, which immediately flipped him and eventually washed him out of his boat. When he reached the bottom, drenched and exhausted, he was not at all pleased with his overly helpful companions and their signaling system.

Group Awareness. Be aware of how everyone is feeling. When people are tired, make camp early. Exhaustion can lead to problems. It is better to quit early and get a good rest than to continue with weary companions.

B.

Kayaks and Rafts Together

When kayakers and rafters travel together on river trips, it normally is best for kayakers to run the rapids first, or, if they follow rafts, to give them plenty of room. Kayakers especially should avoid getting too close to oar rafts that are moving slower than the current because of the back ferrying techniques used. Rafts can knock over kayaks or smash them against rocks, which obviously is something to be avoided.

A group of kayakers that floats ahead of a raft party easily can cover much more ground than the rafters would ever dream of. Tired and sore rafters eventually may catch up with the kayakers, but probably not without a few words of advice for their fleet-floating companions. It is nice for kayakers to break away from rafts from time to time, but they should avoid going too far, both as a safety precaution and as a means of maintaining friendly relationships with their rafting friends.

Occasionally kayakers can lose track of whether rafters are ahead of them or behind. A few years ago, a group of kayakers forged ahead, thinking that the rafters were in front of them. At dark, to their dismay, they realized that the rafts were, in fact, behind them and they were forced to stop for the night. The rafts carried all of their gear and food, and they spent a damp, chilly night in their wet suits.

C.

A system of river signals devised by the American Whitewater Affiliation: Stop (*A*), Help/Emergency (*B*), All Clear (*C*), Come Ahead by This Course (*D*).

River Orientation

Knowing which direction to go on a river is never a problem, but knowing exactly where you are on the river can be another story. Having some idea of where you are is helpful in finding places to camp, locating major rapids, and stopping before you reach falls or other unrunnable sections of the river. The process of river orientation involves periodically

D.

checking your map—the more frequently the map is checked, the better idea you will have of your location, at least in theory.

In this process, it is a great help to keep the map readily accessible. If it is tucked away in the bottom of the kayak storage flotation bag or next to your sleeping bag in the waterproof bag lashed with thirty feet of nylon cord to the raft frame, you probably will not be too enthusiastic about pulling it out. One of the nicest methods for making the map easily accessible is to keep it sealed in a commercially sold waterproof map case or in doubled-up Ziploc plastic bags. Use duct tape to attach the sealed map to the seat of the raft frame or to the deck of the kayak just in front of the cockpit rim—clearly visible, with no mess and no fuss.

The type of map you can use varies, from maps made specially for river running to large-scale maps covering many miles and showing little river detail. Whatever type of map is used, look for clues such as side streams, man-made features, and rapids to help determine position.

Enclosing a map in a waterproof bag and taping it to the bow of the boat is an easy way of keeping a map accessible.

Side Streams.   One of your main clues are side streams or other rivers joining the one you are running. Major side streams that join the river will be indicated as larger blue lines if your map is colored or they will be named on the map. Named features are a key, since most named features on a map are significant and often serve as landmarks to help determine location. As you run the river, note how large each stream is and compare how a stream's size is represented on the map. Later, when you are not sure which stream is which, size may help you make a determination.

Man-Made Features.   If the map is up-to-date, you will be able to identify highway or trail bridges, landing strips, powerline and pipeline crossings, houses near the river, gravel pits, and dams. All are dead giveaways for indicating your position.

Rapids and Falls.   Named rapids and falls along the river help establish location. Topographic maps occasionally show the location of some rapids, but the maps do not necessarily show where all, if any, rapids are located. For locating rapids, by far the best maps are those designed for river running (see the "Guidebooks" section in the "Sources" chapter). When you arrive at significant rapids, you will be able to match them, in most cases, with your river map and get a fix on your location.

Curves.   Every river curves back and forth. With a good map, it is possible to keep track of location by repeatedly referring to the map and keeping track of curves. It is a tedious process, but with a good map it can be done. The process is easiest with large rivers that curve gently. If you keep a compass handy and note your direction, you can cross-check with the direction of the river on the map, further helping to keep yourself oriented. More often, prominent curves are used by boaters: a horseshoe-shaped curve or a very sharp, abrupt corner can be identified on a good map.

Canyons.   Major canyons or gorges that you pass through may be named on maps. When you enter such canyons, check the map and you may be able to pinpoint your location. Flat or swampy areas also may be named or noted.

Surrounding Topography.   Topographic maps that show the lay of the land with contour lines can help provide many clues to location. The easiest way of using a topog map is from a high point above the river, overlooking the surrounding terrain. Climbing above the river, however, is impractical in most cases, but even from a river level, a topog map can be used to identify a number of features and, in turn, help orient you.

Putting It All Together.   The process of orientation on a river does not have to detract from the fun of running the river. It quite often involves simply a quick check of the map. But when you are first learning about orientation or when you are concerned about something coming up, check your map frequently.

Maintaining an awareness of location actually involves some or all of the previously discussed clues. As you run the river, watch for side streams and note the side on which they enter, be aware of any man-made features, and keep track of the surrounding topography and other clues. Form a mental image of your observations and use the map to orient yourself. The process is continuous. As you pick up new information, revise and reorient yourself. Enjoy your companions and the river experience, but at the same time keep the back of your mind alert to a sense of where you are.

Running Rapids

Before entering a rapid, rafters and kayakers should prepare as though the boat will flip. Rafters should be certain that life jackets are securely fastened, lines have not come undone so they could entangle legs, and any loose items are packed away. Passengers in an oar raft can help by bailing if the boat takes on water going through the rapid. In smaller oar rafts and paddle rafts, riders can help by shifting weight to the high side if the boat begins to tip. Kayakers should prepare themselves by being sure the spray skirt is fastened, the helmet is snugly strapped, and the life jacket is secure.

Contour lines spaced close together indicate steep canyon areas. The closer together the lines, the steeper the canyon.

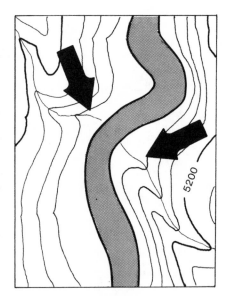

V-shaped contour lines pointing away from each other on opposite sides of the river indicate side drainages entering on opposite sides of the river.

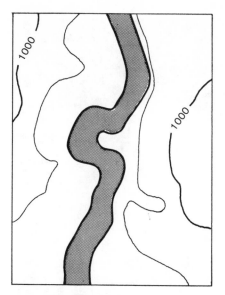

Contour lines spaced far apart indicate that the terrain surrounding this portion of the river changes fairly gradually.

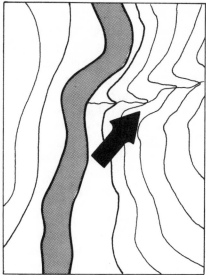

V-shaped contour lines with the apex of the V pointing away from the river indicate a stream drainage. The stream drainage shown in this example is relatively small.

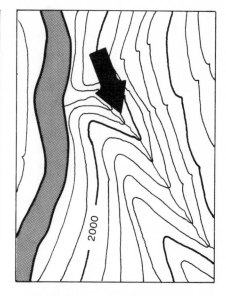

The sharper and more pronounced the V-shaped contour lines, the more prominent is the stream drainage. In this example, a stream enters the river in a larger side drainage than shown in the preceding illustration.

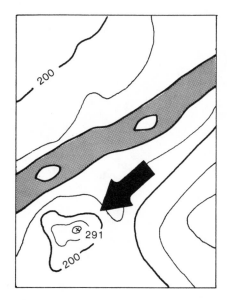

Prominent landmarks such as hills and peaks are not always visible from the river because of the limited view of the low vantage point. But now and then, you may have views of nearby or distant points. In this example, contour lines forming circles inside one another, spaced relatively far apart, indicate a gradually sloped hill.

Circular or closed contour lines made within each other and spaced close together indicate a rugged peak.

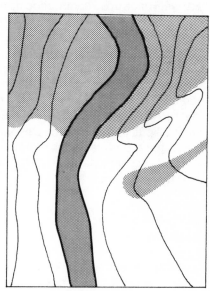

Topographic maps also may indicate forested areas by a green or gray shading. The river runner may be able to determine position as he leaves or enters an area of forestation.

Scouting

As you run a river, always look ahead to ascertain the difficulty of coming rapids. Continue paddling or oaring through a rapid if it looks well within your ability and you see a good eddy to pull into at the bottom.

If there is any question, however, stop and get out of the boat to take a look from land. This process of looking at a rapid from along the shore is known as scouting. Unfortunately, from the level of a boat, you cannot get a very good look of what surprises may be hidden in a rapid. Large, boat-flipping holes may be disguised by waves, or a channel that looks clean from above may be blocked by treacherous boulders farther downstream. By scouting from the shore you can locate the bad places and plan a safe route.

Do not run anything you cannot see. A blind corner, a series of large rocks, the severe drop of the rapid itself may obstruct the view of an awesome rapid. All you may be able to see are the tops of boulders and water splashing. Whenever you have any uncertainty about what lies below, pull off and take a look.

In the next three chapters, more information will be covered on how to read and run rapids. While scouting you basically are looking for the best passage through a particular rapid. The place where you enter the rapid is important. As you look it over, paint a mental picture of what you see and try to imagine what it will look like from the seat of your boat. As you walk back upstream, notice how the rocks now appear from your new upstream view. They will look different, and in some cases, it is essential that you know which rock is which. If you are confused by your new view from upstream, scramble back to a location alongside the rapid to recheck. Do not begin your run until you are sure.

Use landmarks in the rapid to help guide you. For instance, you may use a large, flat boulder at the top of the rapid for entry: "I'll enter three feet to the right of that boulder. Once I'm past the downed tree on the left bank, I'll pull to the far right. Beyond the cliff, I'll turn the boat straight to avoid going broadside through the holes at the bottom." Also, keep in mind an alternate plan: "If I blow it here, which route should I follow to get past that nasty hole?"

Scouting a rapid

Lining

If after scouting the rapid you decide there is no possible or safe way to run it, you will have to decide on a method of getting your boat around. The easiest method is to line the boat. Lining is done with rafts, dories, and other large boats. Kayakers may be able to do a simple type of lining by holding onto the grab loop and floating the boat alongside the shore in shallow water, dragging it over rocks, and if necessary, picking it up and carrying it around any section where the water is too swift.

Lining is most valuable with heavily loaded rafts where portaging would mean backbreaking work, carrying the boat and gear around the rapid.

One boat at a time is lined so everyone in a party is available to help in the process, during which each person continues to wear his life jacket. To line, use two strong ropes that are tied to the front and back of the boat. One or more people can help hold the lines. The idea is to nudge the boat along by pulling on the front rope, or to stand in the water, if this is safe,

Lining a raft

and push by hand. Keep the boat fairly close to shore where it can be handled, working it around larger rocks and through chutes by floating, and sometimes dragging, it past the unrunnable portion of the rapid.

In some situations, you may be forced to move the boat farther away from the bank to negotiate a passageway. Once the boat is through, quickly pull it back in toward the bank so that it is not washed farther out into the rapid where it would be difficult to control. Whenever you use ropes, and especially when the boat is in fast water, use extreme caution. Do not allow the rope to become tangled around your legs or body, and do not wrap the rope around your hand. Use gloves to prevent rope burn.

If you reach a portion of the rapid where the boat is able to float freely downstream, position the boat at a forty-five-degree angle so that the back end is angled out into the current. The position will help push the boat along. But do not allow the boat to get broadside during any of the lining process. Once broadside, the boat is vulnerable to getting pinned against rocks.

When a boat floats freely, the lining process may go easier if the boat is kept at a forty-five-degree angle to the bank.

If it is safe, one or more people can walk beside the boat, helping to lift and pull it over rocks. Use caution whenever walking in rivers. If a foot is caught, even in shallow swift water, you quickly can be pulled and held under. Lining is wet, hard work—shoving, bouncing, and yanking the boat over shallows and rocks—but in the long run, it is easier than the next method—portaging.

Portaging

The following river and terrain features may prevent you from lining:
- Vertical cliffs may rise up from either side of the river.
- A falls may drop too steeply.
- The rapid may not have any weakness or slower moving water along either of its sides.
- Trees may be down all the way across the river.

In any of these cases you will be forced to portage. A portage may not be too much of a problem—just carrying a kayak around a tree, for example—or a portage may be difficult—trudging for several miles over cliffs and through brush, swamps, and other obstacles. Popular rivers usually have short portages or none at all, but occasionally some boaters, to get away from the crowds, purposely seek out rivers with long portages.

If you know you might have to portage, the situation can be helped by keeping weight to a minimum. Various river bags with shoulder straps help expedite the portaging process. When I know I will be portaging, I always take along a large-capacity backpack, which makes carrying the gear easier.

Kayak Portaging.   To portage a kayak, use any one of the following suggestions:
- If the portage is short, such as with a quick carry around a downed tree across the river, leave the gear in the boat, hoist the kayak so that the cockpit rim is on your shoulder, and carry the boat around.
- Have another person help you if the kayak is too heavy or the portage is longer. He can hold the front grab loop while you grab the back one. Two people are particularly helpful for carrying a kayak up steep embankments or over huge boulders or other difficult obstacles.
- If the terrain is not too rough, the process can be expedited by the two boaters carrying two boats, each grabbing a grab loop of each boat in his hands. Sticks can be placed through the bow and stern grab loops to make gripping easier.
- For really long portages over rugged terrain, I carry an internal frame pack inside the boat. After I put all the gear in the pack, I either carry both the boat and the pack, or first carry the pack around and return to get the boat.

Raft Portaging.   Here are some possible methods you may use for portaging an inflatable raft:
- If the boat and gear are not too heavy, the entire boat, left inflated, may be picked up by several people and carried around.
- If the boat and gear are heavy, unload the boat and carry the gear around. Then carry the boat around. Often it is easiest to leave the boat inflated and portage it in rigid form. Other times,

On a short portage, a kayak can be carried on the boater's shoulder. (The kayaker on the ground is practicing a sand roll.)

Two people carrying one kayak makes portage less difficult.

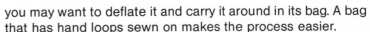

Sticks placed through the grab loops make it easier to keep a grip while portaging two boats.

Deflating a raft, wrapping it around the oars, and carrying it like a stretcher is another method of portaging.

you may want to deflate it and carry it around in its bag. A bag that has hand loops sewn on makes the process easier.

- Boats often are unwieldy and difficult to carry, even in a storage bag. If that is the case, deflate the boat and fold it around two oars or two long sturdy sticks, creating something that looks similar to a stretcher. One person in front can grab the oars or sticks in each hand while the other grips the rear, and the boat is carried like a stretcher.

Friendly Gestures

Various conflicts can occur between different parties on rivers, among the members within the group, and with private owners of property along the river. In some places such as the western United States, boaters are fortunate to have many rivers flowing through public land. But in many other locations, much of the riverbank may be owned by private individuals. If you must cross or camp on private land, always obtain permission in advance. Go out of your way to be friendly to the landowner. Pick up garbage on his property, and warn others if you see any type of abuse occurring. Unfortunately, in a number of areas boaters

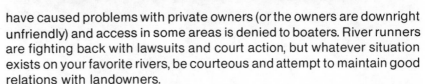

have caused problems with private owners (or the owners are downright unfriendly) and access in some areas is denied to boaters. River runners are fighting back with lawsuits and court action, but whatever situation exists on your favorite rivers, be courteous and attempt to maintain good relations with landowners.

Another conflict that has occurred on rivers is between boaters and fishermen. Give fishermen a wide berth as you float by them and warn others in the party to do the same.

If other parties catch up to your group, give them room if they wish to pass. Kayakers should give the boat downstream of them the right-of-way and not crowd it. When playing in waves, be careful not to surf out in front of another kayaker coming down the river. After you have surfed, move out of the way and let the others try it before you go again.

On warm, wilderness rivers, some boaters enjoy slipping out of clothing and stretching out in the nude. If hot springs are located on the river, it is traditional to strip down and soak. Be aware, though, that nudity, while perfectly natural in wild places where people are free of the restrictions of society, can be distasteful to other groups on the river, and boaters should be discreet while frolicking.

Portaging an inflated raft

READING WHITE WATER

Walt turned behind the eddy and broke out on the other side, neatly missing an ominous jagged rock against which the current was slamming. I followed his moves, turning in one side of the eddy and out the other, avoiding the rock. We plunged over a small falls, sliding down a slick of water and escaping the mean, foaming holes on either side. I continued following Walt's zigzag pattern, missing rocks, catching eddies, and slipping through narrow chutes. As far as I could see, boulder-choked rapids stretched in front of us, and we continued hopping eddies, looking ahead, and darting from side to side for eight glorious miles.

Unfortunately, I had only a few chances to boat with the late Walt Blackadar, a master and promoter of big water kayaking. He was well known for his extraordinary exploits of the Alsek River in Canada, but the tumbling mountain stream we ran together was small and rocky. He was far from being a graceful or smooth boater, but he had developed the art of reading water to a fine degree. For the eight fast-paced miles, I continually was amazed how he could look ahead, detect small currents and eddies, and use them to put himself, with a minimum of effort, where he wanted to go.

To run rapids successfully, you do not have to read white water as keenly as Walt did, but you do need to develop a basic sense and understanding of river current peculiarities. Reading white water is comparable to picking a route on a road map to reach a destination. The object of running a rapid is to reach the bottom safely, which may involve taking any number of routes. To begin to understand how to read the road map of rapids, let's start with some basic terms.

Basic Terms

Rivers, of course, flow from higher to lower elevations. The direction that you travel is *downstream*. The direction you have come from is *upstream*. A rock protruding from the surface of the river has a downstream side—the side facing downstream—and an upstream side—the side facing upstream. A boat turned sideways in the current has one side facing downstream and one side facing upstream. *Left* and *right* sides

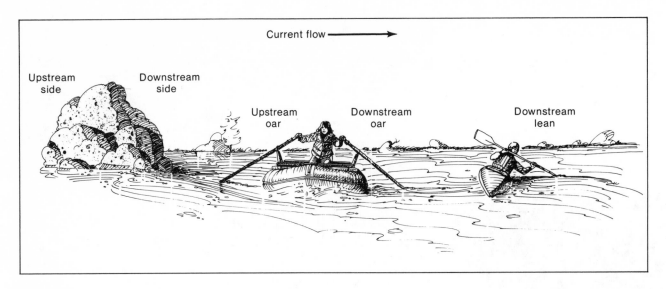

Current flow ⟶

Upstream side   Downstream side   Upstream oar   Downstream oar   Downstream lean

are as you would view the river facing downstream.

Upstream and downstream (*side view*)

Straight Stretch

Water flowing down a straight stretch of a river of uniform depth is slowed due to friction caused by the water moving against the bed and bank of the river. Because of this friction, the current flow generally is greatest in the middle of the river near the surface of the water.

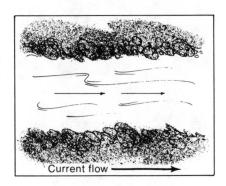

Current flow ⟶

Straight stretch (*top view*). Friction on the sides of a river slows the current, so the fastest water is in the middle.

Bends

Rivers, of course, do not flow straight for long. Taking the line of least resistance, they bend and twist and snake their way to lower ground. In a sharp bend, the current tends to flow straight, creating a greater flow of current on the outside of the bend. The outside of the bend, then, has the faster current and deeper water, while the inside has the slower current.

The slower current on the inside of the bend allows sediment carried by the river to be dropped, and in many rivers, a gravel or sand bar is formed. The faster, more forceful current on the outside of the bend erodes the bank. Often, you will find steep embankments or rocky cliffs on the outside of the curves. If trees are growing there, the bank eventually may cave in and cause the trees to topple in the water. Therefore, the outside of curves are common places to find tree hazards.

On sharp curves, a boater normally enters on the inside. If the outside looks free of overhanging trees and other white-water difficulties, he easily can move to the outside. If he is trying to make time, the outside of the curve offers the faster current.

However, if he sees a downed tree or some hazardous boulders on the outside of the bend, by pulling into the slower current of the inside he can stop, scout if necessary, or ease around the obstacle in a safe and controlled manner. If he starts on the outside, the natural tendency of the current to keep him on the outside may prevent him from escaping to the relatively quieter water on the inside.

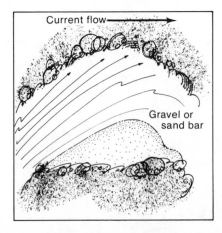

Current flow ⟶

Gravel or sand bar

Bend (*top view*). The fastest water is found on the outside of a bend.

Bend with gravel bar on the inside

Current flow ⟶

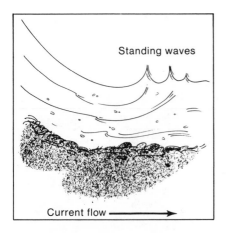

Standing waves form from dissipated energy when water slows (*side view*).

Rapids or Drops

Most rapids exist because, in a short distance, the river is losing significant elevation. Generally, the more elevation lost per distance traveled, the more difficult is the rapid. Because of this loss of elevation, rapids often are referred to as *drops*.

The drop of a rapid is one of the reasons why it is important to stop and scout it. When you view a rapid from a position above it and *on the water*, the elevation loss may be great enough to prevent you from seeing all the obstacles.

Near the end of a long drop the water, bristling with energy, meets the low energy water, causing the formation of regular- or nearly regular-shaped waves known as *standing waves* or *haystacks*. The standing waves can vary considerably in size, but the largest wave usually is found at the base of the drop, followed by other standing waves, with each succeeding wave decreasing in size.

Unless the standing waves are extremely large, their regular shape does not threaten boaters and provides much of the excitement in river running. Rafters love to ride them, enjoying the roller coaster ride. Often, even the huge standing waves are fun, lifting a boat high in the air and plunging it down in a trough and then up again.

Kayakers use standing waves for gliding from one side of the river to the other. A standing wave that is symmetrically shaped across part or all of the river is a special treat. Paddling upstream in the wave, a kayaker can achieve a state of equilibrium as the bow is pulled down the upstream face of the wave by gravity. The downstream flow of water balances the effect of gravity and keeps the kayak in the same place. This exhilarating technique, known as *surfing*, poses the kayaker on a wave while the current rushes by on either side.

Constrictions

In places where the river converges sharply, the current accelerates through the constriction. Just below the constriction, the fast-moving water slows, and as it loses energy, a series of standing waves often results. These regular-shaped waves usually are some of the nicest

Current flow ⟶

Standing wave with kayak on end

waves for kayak surfing.

Rocks above the Water Surface

Rocks, boulders, and any other obstructions such as a bridge pier that protrude above the surface of the river block the normal flow of current. Water collides with the upstream face of the rock, rebounds, and spills to either side. The area on the upstream side of the rock where water piles up is known as the *cushion*. With a small volume of water and slow current, the cushion may be barely noticeable. With larger volumes and stronger current, the cushion may be impressive. Midway down one of the most famous drops in the United States, Lava Falls on the Colorado River, is a huge chunk of basalt. The current slams against the basalt and rebounds, creating a huge cushion. On my one raft run of Lava Falls, our boat was thrown helplessly at the dark foreboding rock. About a yard away, however, the boat hit the cushion and to our relief, bounced up and back into the current, still right side up.

As the water slides around either side of a protruding rock, it fills in the gap left downstream of the rock. The water pouring in downstream of the rock creates an upstream flow of current, which is known as an *eddy*. An eddy behind a rock can be barely noticeable in low volumes of water and slow current, or extremely powerful in greater volumes of water and faster current.

Eddies also can form because of irregularities in the riverbank. For example, a boulder jutting out from the bank creates an eddy behind it. Eddies also can be found at the bottom of a constriction, described in the previous section.

Eddies are one of the more useful hydraulic formations in a river. Along the bank, boaters use them as stopping places in fast water. In mid-river, rafters use eddies behind rocks to slow themselves down or to assist them in making moves from one side to another. Kayakers and canoeists extensively use eddies—turning into them, stopping in them, and turning out of them. A kayaker slowly may work his way down a rapid, darting back and forth from eddy to eddy.

The transition zone between the downstream flow of the current and the upstream flow of the eddy is called the *eddy line*. In high water, this

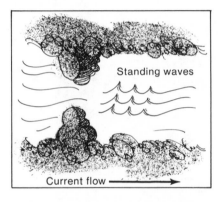

Standing waves often are found just below a constriction
(*top view*).

Current flow ⟶

Constriction formed by large boulders on both sides of the river (*top view*). Note the two well-defined standing waves (indicated by two lines of white) formed just below the constriction.

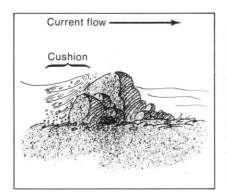

A cushion forms on the upstream side of an obstruction (*side view*).

This large cushion on the upstream side of the large boulder is pushing the raft around to the boater's left. As the water level drops, the cushion will become less pronounced.

Current flow ⟶

Current flow ⟶

Eddies form on the downstream side of rocks.

Eddies form in a variety of places. *Top view, from left*: behind irregularities in the riverbank (*A*), behind a rock (*B*), and at the bottom of a constriction (*C*).

transition zone can become a confusing mixture of swirling, swelling currents. A boat in the midst of the eddy line in high, large-volume water can be tossed and spun about. Kayakers find it difficult to stay right side up with currents pushing randomly from different sides. Boaters usually try to build up momentum to try to break and pass quickly through such eddy lines. Because eddy lines are turbulent in high water, some boaters refer to them as *eddy walls*.

Whether in low or high water, the eddy line separates the current flowing in two different directions: one upstream and one downstream. If the bow of a boat is in an eddy and the stern is in the main current, the two opposing current flows will cause the boat to spin. An experienced boater can preplan a spin and use it to his advantage, but quite often new boaters unknowingly will nose into an eddy and get spun around and thrown off course. As you run a river, watch for eddies and position your boat so you are not caught by surprise and spun around.

Reading Hints for Eddies. Eddies form behind rocks in midriver or behind rocks jutting out from the riverbank. The larger the rock, the larger the eddy behind it. Eddies may be visible by outward signs of upstream current movement, such as bubbles or pieces of debris floating upstream. Use eddies for stopping and/or making moves, as described in the chapters about kayak and raft techniques.

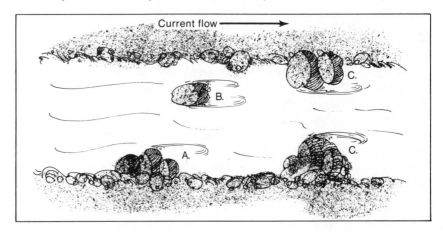

Rocks under the Water Surface

A rock just under the surface of the river causes the water to rise up and over it, forming a smooth bump called a *pillow*. If the rock is in fairly shallow water, the water immediately after it will drop sharply and form a curling-back, foamy patch. When you view a rapid, the patches of foam indicate rocks located just upstream under the water. Avoid rocks that are close to the surface, because they can cause damage, especially if they are sharp, to both rafts and kayaks, or sometimes can cause boats to get snagged and held in midstream.

When a rock is a little farther beneath the water surface, the foam gives way to a standing wave (or several waves) behind the rock. The deeper the rock, the farther downstream the standing wave forms. In this case, a kayaker may be able to float over the rock without scraping the boat. Rafters may or may not scrape, depending on how deep their boat

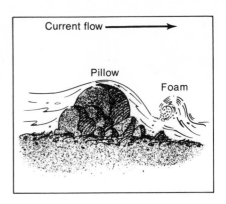

A rock located just under the water surface is indicated by a pillow and a patch of foam behind it (*side view*).

A hump or pillow forms over a rock and a curling-back patch of foamy water forms just behind it.

Current flow ⟶

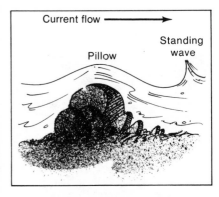

A standing wave forms beyond a pillow when a rock is located well below the water surface (*side view*).

sinks in the water.

Reading Hints.   Look for the hump of water or pillow and a patch of foam behind it. The pillow is where the rock is located. In clear water, you can see the dark color of the rock under the pillow to help you further distinguish it. If the water is dirty, you will have to use the pillow-foam configuration for identification.

Formation of Vs

If, from a position above the river, you look down on rocks just under or protruding from the surface of the water, you can see a V or U shape pointing upstream which is formed by foam, ripples, or eddy lines. The rock is located in the tip of the V or U. If two rocks are located across from each other, two tails of the Vs will cross, forming a second V, the tip of which points downstream.

This downstream V points to the passageway between two rocks while the upstream V indicates rocks located in its apex.

Often the start of a rapid is marked by downstream Vs. Several of

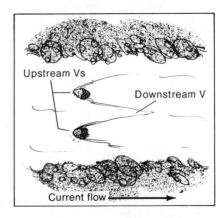

Upstream Vs or Us are formed by rocks protruding from or just below the surface of the water. A downstream V forms between two rocks (*side view*).

Current flow ⟶

Downstream Vs at the beginning of rapids sometimes are called tongues or chutes.

them may be present and based on what the rest of the rapid is like, choose the V that starts you in the most advantageous position. Boaters often refer to downstream Vs at the beginning of rapids as *tongues* or *chutes.*

Reading Hints. Vs are visible when viewed from the side or above the river. Look for foam, ripples, or waves that outline the V. An upstream V indicates that a rock is located in its tip. The rocks may be showing or just under the surface of the water. The downstream V indicates the passageway between two rocks. Vs are most useful at the beginning of a rapid. Farther down in a rapid, increased turbulence may hide where the Vs are located and other reading methods come into play to determine the correct route.

Holes

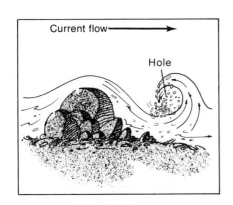

Hole formed behind a rock (*side view*)

We have looked at the situation in which a rock is located just below the water's surface. The water pouring over the rock and curling back creates a patch of foam. The term *hole* refers to the depression just behind the rock. Normally, boaters loosely define holes as situations in which the rock under the water surface is large and the volume of water dropping over it is great. Holes have the capability of stopping the forward momentum of boats, flipping them over, or in some cases, entrapping the boat by the violently curling-back, foamy water.

Holes also are called souse holes, hydraulics, reversals, vertical eddies, and stoppers. Some boaters attach different meanings to the terms, but since differences are not totally clear among river runners, I will keep it simple and refer to the general phenomenon as a hole, and will more specifically refer to the dangerous circulating hole formed below dams and weirs as a *hydraulic.*

Current flow ⟶

This particular hole has a long stretch of recirculating water that tends to catch and hold kayaks and rafts for awhile.

Looking at the illustration of a hole, you can see that the water near the surface of the river is curling back upstream, forming the turbulence of the hole. Lying deeper underneath the surface of the river is a current that flows downstream. The current may be useful to an unfortunate boater who is trapped in a hole. If he is in his boat, he may be able to plunge his oar or paddle deep enough to catch the downstream current to help pull him out. Or if he is out of his boat, swimming and caught in a hole, his feet may sink deep enough to catch the downstream current.

Holes also are created by some large waves that are unable to support the weight of water. The water crashes back down the face of the wave, creating a recirculating foamy patch of water.

The smaller holes can be run with little problem. They may slow the boat a tad, and kayakers may get splashed, but in most cases they present few problems. The exception to this is the hole created by a dam or weir, discussed in the next section.

The larger holes, however, normally are avoided unless the boater is experienced. To avoid large holes, make moves early enough in the rapid to get away from them. If you find yourself in a wrong position and must run a bad hole, the technique used by most boaters is to point the boat straight ahead and paddle or oar hard to gain momentum to carry you through the foaming wave, which is slapping back upstream.

Reading Hints.   Big patches of white indicate holes. A clue to help you identify a hole while in your boat is *discontinuities* in the rapid ahead. Scan the rapid, watching closely for an area in which a *calm spot* or a *horizontal line* seems to exist in the midst of turbulence. A hole may be located there. As you float closer, look for the smooth pillow. Behind the pillow, some of the white of the foaming portion of the hole may be visible. On big holes, however, the foam may not be visible until you are dropping over the edge.

When the hole is not visible, you sometimes may be able to detect vaporous air just above the hole. The mist is caused by fine droplets of water thrown into the air by the crashing, boiling water.

Since holes are not always readily identifiable when trying to locate them from in a boat, scouting major rapids and anything you cannot see clearly is always the best procedure.

In a downstream view of a rapid, a horizontal line or calm spot often indicates the location of a hole.

From upstream, holes sometimes are detectable because of a mist that hangs over a horizontal line.

Current flow ⟶

Ledges and Dams

One type of hole or hydraulic that even very experienced boaters avoid is one formed behind a symmetrical obstruction underneath the surface of the water. A dam or weir usually is the culprit, forming a hole that extends all the way across the river. The water drops over the dam and circulates around and around in the foamy area below the dam. A person who floats over it can be caught and held in the backwash, which extends several feet out from the base of the dam. It is only when a boat or person reaches the darker-colored water below the dam that any downstream current is encountered. Relatively harmless dams only a few feet high can create a deathtrap hole at the bottom. Rescuers of people caught in the backwash behind dams have been pulled into the hydraulic and drowned along with the victims. If you ever help someone caught below a dam, always keep your boat in the darker, downstream

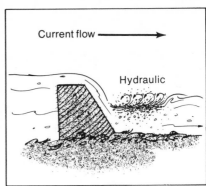

Hydraulic at base of dam (*side view*)

Victims trapped in the powerful hydraulic formed below a dam only a couple of feet high. Note the other debris also held by the hydraulic. The boat trapped in the background is still upright, but it capsized after the photo was taken. The victims were rescued successfully.

water. The white, bubble-laden water is part of the dangerous upstream current creating the hole.

Fortunately, natural obstructions in rivers are not so symmetrical as man-made structures. Occasionally, however, the riverbed may consist of ledges that have broken off squarely. Symmetrical hydraulics can form behind them. Although rare, they should be avoided when encountered.

Reading Hints. The trouble with dams and ledges is that they are extremely difficult to identify from upstream while floating on the river. There may be no sound and no visible white splashing in the air. Even experienced boaters can miss them. Scan the river in front of you, searching for a *horizontal line* that forms at the edge of dams. Look ahead at features on the shore. If the tops of trees are visible ahead but not the bottom portions, stop and take a look. A sudden quickening of current may indicate that you are just above the dam. Because dams can sneak up on you, you may not detect one until you are a few feet away. That does not give you enough time to get to shore and you may go over sideways in your attempt to get there. Instead, in the few moments that you have, look for a nick or some break in the symmetrical top of the dam. There may be one a few feet to either side of your path and just a few moments may be enough time for you to stroke once or twice to get in the nick and wash through the hydraulic at the base of the dam.

Strainers

Strainers are anything in the river that allows water, but not a body or boat, to pass through. Trees and brush in the river are the most common strainers, but undercut boulders, split rocks, and bridge piers that are close together have the same effect. Strainers are extremely dangerous. A boater swept into a tree can be held until he drowns. *Avoid them at all costs.*

Reading Hints. Always keep an eye out for downed trees on any river. Small, narrow rivers are most susceptible to trees blocking the

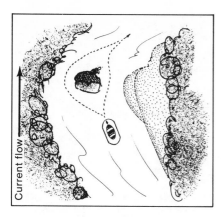

In this example (*top view*), taking the strongest current, which is to the left of the boulder, is the boater's easier option. If he were to go to the right, the current could force him into the boulder.

entire channel. The undercutting action of water on the outside of curves can knock trees into the river. Enter curves on the inside, and do not run anything you cannot see.

Path of Greatest Current

Every rapid has areas of stronger and weaker currents. When scouting a rapid, look for the path of the strongest current. You may or may not be able to use the strong current to help you get through the rapid. On some rivers, the strongest current can be very powerful and once in it, trying to fight it can be fruitless.

If the main current leads into hazards, you will want to avoid it. Note its location and plan a careful route to avoid its effects as much as possible.

An example where the boater can be helped by using the strongest current is shown in the path of greatest current illustration. He can go right or left to miss a mean boulder in the middle of the river. Because of the curvature of the river, the strongest current flows to the left of the rock. Since no obstacles exist beyond the rock, the left side is the boater's best choice. A boater also could go to the right, which might be entirely possible, but an extremely strong current could sweep him to the left, perhaps even throwing him against the very rock he is trying to avoid.

Reading Hints. To determine the strongest current, look at the rapid. Look for places where the current is deep and swift. Larger waves form in the deeper, swifter channels. Look at the cushions in front of rocks protruding above the surface. Larger cushions indicate greater water volumes and stronger currents. If the rapid is located on a corner, the stronger current often flows toward the outside.

Increased Water Volume

In high water, a number of things happen: standing waves get bigger, eddy lines become more turbulent, and eddy currents get stronger. In high water some holes are covered by increased water volume and may turn into standing waves. With even more water, the hole may be completely washed out. But new holes also are formed and are more violent. A river in higher flows is more challenging but also more dangerous, and boaters need to use extra caution.

Reading Hints. Higher flows on river are signaled by water levels that are close to or actually flowing into the trees and bushes alongside the river. Debris floating down the river signal high flows. The river also may be muddy (but not always), and the current is fast.

Classification of White Water

To provide a basis of comparison between rapids and the difficulty of rivers, the American Whitewater Affiliation has borrowed from the Europeans and promoted in North America a scale of I through VI. The scale has gained wide acceptance in most areas of North America. The description that follows explains the characteristics of each of the categories. You should remember that no matter how a particular rapid is rated, the rating can change. In high water, a class II rapid can turn into a nightmare. In addition, the river can change. A tree may fall across it or a landslide may completely alter an easy stretch. Trust your own judgment by scouting the rapid before deciding to run it.

Rapids of the same classification may vary widely. Some rapids may be shallow and require rock dodging while others might be deep with large waves and holes. Run different types of rapids of the same classification before moving up. Rapids harder than class IV are extremely difficult and involve serious risks. Most boaters are happy with class IV and below.

Class I. This is basically flat water, though it also may have some small waves and ripples. It is the best place to learn white-water techniques and to familiarize yourself with your craft. In high water, however, some class I stretches can be difficult and even dangerous for beginners. It is best to save trips for when the water is down.

Class II. The easiest rapids are found under this classification. Waves can get up to about three feet high. Scouting is not necessary. Channels are obvious.

Class III. These are moderately hard rapids. The boatman should know the basics of reading water and respond with correct turns and moves to work his way through rapids. Rapids may contain numerous boulders and holes that could flip a kayak or canoe and occasionally some rafts. Maneuvering is required to miss rocks and holes. Scouting is helpful for inexperienced boaters to plan their route. More experienced boaters may be able to scout from the river as they run through it.

Class I water

Class II rapid

Class III rapid

Class IV. Skillful maneuvering is required in running the rocky, constricted channels of these difficult rapids. They may contain large holes that can flip any craft. Kayakers should know how to roll. In most cases, class IV drops should be scouted.

Class V. These extremely difficult, violent, turbulent rapids may require complicated maneuvering through rock mazes. Holes can be huge, unrelenting, difficult to avoid, and able to flip the largest of white-water craft. Usually class V rapids are the domain of kayaks and decked canoes, but they sometimes are run by rubber boats. Kayakers and decked canoe boaters must be able to execute a reliable roll. Rescue is

very difficult and when it is possible, the probability of injury or death from an accident or swim is high.

Class VI.   Some boaters term this classification as unrunnable. Most sources define it as class V, carried to nightmarish extremes. Some people classify boaters who attempt rapids in this range as daredevils, paddling a thin line between life and death. Pete Skinner of the American Whitewater Affiliation (West Sand Lake, New York) emphasizes that class VI has a high likelihood of injury or death.

Class IV rapid

Class V rapid

Class VI rapid

KAYAK TECHNIQUE

I never thought that George would ever join me on another river trip. On our first trip, I had helped line up an inflatable raft for him and three other friends from Michigan to use. The thin, yellow, rubberized, cotton Taiwan raft was not the best for white water, but it was all that was available. Early in the trip the raft floor ripped from bow to stern in a rapid, and George and his friends fell through the bottom of the boat into the chilly river. After patching the boat, they managed with painstaking care to nurse it down the remainder of the river.

The next summer, after a highly regimented year of an orthopedic internship, George was ready for more. This time, however, he brought his own boat: a kayak. His experience with the kayak on rivers was limited, but he did find time from his medical responsibilities to get into a swimming pool and learn how to roll.

The river we planned to run was the Selway, an Idaho wilderness river with big drops and powerful holes. It was a lofty challenge for George, but he wanted to give it a try. The three other, more experienced kayakers along on the trip were skeptical when they learned he was coming.

Drenching rains that hammered at us every day on the Selway brought the river level up. The rapids hammered at us harder, flipping rafts and kayaks alike. Two of the kayakers took bad swims, and one of the kayaks was battered and smashed against rocks. A long, chilly evening was spent under a pack bridge trying to repair the damage.

Despite the problems that many of the others were having, George came through all the rapids right side up and in his boat. Though his style was not the smoothest, his roll was reliable and whenever he was knocked over he determinedly rolled back up.

George's success on the Selway demonstrates the importance of the roll. Even though his experience was limited, the roll gave him confidence to run rapids without worrying about taking energy-sapping swims. When he practiced techniques on the river and was tipped over, he could right himself.

I do not want to minimize the importance of starting out with easy rapids and gradually developing skills and the ability to run white water. On the contrary, developing a good roll *in combination with* progressing slowly from easier to harder rapids is by far the best method of learning. If you are just beginning kayaking or have not learned the roll, make it a priority to get in a pool or lake and start working on the technique. With the roll, you will be safer, and everything you learn on the river will come quicker. Before discussing the roll, let's begin with a few basics.

Where to Practice

Developing skills in a kayak begins on easy water where you can practice some of the basics. In fact, the best place to start is in a swimming pool or on a warm lake on hot summer days. At first you will flounder around trying strokes and practicing the roll, and it is nice to start some place where it is warm. In a comfortable water environment, you can learn quicker and be ready to tackle the river sooner.

Work with a friend or attend pool sessions offered by various white-water clubs and organizations. They can help immensely. The way the techniques—especially the roll—are presented in this chapter has worked well with the hundreds of people I have worked with in kayak classes. Individuals, however, learn skills by different methods, and other sources and teaching methods may be of great help while you are learning. Some excellent sources include: *Kayaking* by Jay Evans, *White Water Handbook* by John Urban (revised by T. Walley Williams), and *Wild-Water Canoeing and Kayaking* by Robert Steidle (see the "Books" section in the "Sources" chapter).

To get into a kayak, hold it against a rock or the riverbank, place your paddle as shown to keep the boat from pushing away from you, and straighten your legs as you lower yourself in.

First Steps

If you never have climbed into a kayak while in the water, it is good to know a few pointers. With the kayak in the water against the side of a pool or bank of a river, place the paddle behind you, holding with one hand the shaft of the paddle and the cockpit rim of the boat. Use the paddle resting on the side of the pool or bank of the river to keep the boat upright and from pushing away from you as you get in. Straighten your legs and slip in.

To be sure you easily can get out of the boat, flip it over, relax, and drop out of the boat. Do it a couple of times without a spray skirt, and then with a spray skirt, until you feel comfortable. Some people refer to this as the "wet exit." Remember, when you use a spray skirt, always keep the shock cord ends or webbing on top and ready to be pulled if for any reason the spray skirt should bind you while you are getting out of the boat.

Paddling

After you feel confident that you easily can get out of your kayak, try paddling. Since the paddle blades are set at right angles to one another, you need to turn the paddle shaft a half twist with each stroke. One of your hands grasps the shaft and makes this twist (this is called the *grip hand*) while the other hand allows the shaft to slide. If you use a curved-bladed paddle and grip the paddle with your right hand, you need to use a right grip paddle, and vice versa if you grip with your left hand. Practice paddling forward and backward.

As you spend more days in a kayak, paddling will become more comfortable and you may want to begin to work on some of the finer points of paddling. Many recreational boaters do not worry too much about their paddling style, which is fine, but for those wishing to develop a more efficient style, here are a few pointers:

- Sit in the boat with a slight lean and reach with the right blade, fully extending the right arm and shoulder. The left elbow is at shoulder height and the left hand is at eye level.
- Pull the right blade through the water. As the blade moves through the water, twist the body. The stroke is completed when the right elbow reaches the hip. As you pull the right blade, the left arm pushes forward in a punching motion. At the end of the stroke the left shoulder is extended.
- Continue the stroke by slipping the right blade out of the water and bringing the right hand to eye level. The movement dips the left blade in the water, and the stroke continues on the left side, then right, then left, fluidly.

Payson Kennedy of the Nantahala Outdoor Center (Bryson City, North Carolina) places much of the emphasis of forward paddling on flexibility. He recommends loosening and relaxing the upper body and rotating at the waist as you reach out to do each stroke.

Definition of Power Face

For much of the discussion that follows, the term *power face* needs special mention. The power face is the face of the paddle that is pulled against the water in a forward stroke. In other words, it is the face of the blade that faces toward the rear or stern of your kayak as you make a forward stroke. If you are using a curved-bladed paddle, the power face is the concave side of the blade.

Draw Strokes

To do a draw stroke on the right side, reach out with the right blade of the paddle on the right side of the kayak. With the power face turned so it is parallel to the boat and facing you, pull it straight toward you until it is next to the boat. The entire boat will move to the right. If you continue to do draw strokes on the right, the boat can be moved sideways all the way across the pool, lake, or river on which you are practicing. Try doing draw strokes on both sides. One hint that will make things a little easier is that after you pull the blade in next to the boat, turn it perpendicular to the boat and it will slip out of the water easily so you can reach out and make the next draw stroke.

You also can make a draw stroke by placing the right blade in the water a few feet off the right side of your bow and pulling the power face of the blade into the bow. This *bow draw* will turn the bow of the boat to the right. Try the bow draw on both the right and left sides. The bow draw can be combined with other strokes, particularly with the Duffek (explained later in the "Eddies" section) to make effective maneuvers on the river.

Sweep Strokes

The most effective stroke for turning your kayak is the sweep stroke. To do a *forward sweep* on the right side, place the right blade of the paddle in the water near the bow of your boat. *The power face of the blade*

A.

B.

C.

D.

Sweep strokes frequently are used in kayaking to turn the kayak. A *forward sweep* done on the right side, as illustrated, will turn the bow of the kayak to the left. Place the right blade near the bow as in (*A*). Sweep the blade in a wide arc from the front to back (*B, C, D*).

A reverse sweep done on the right side will turn the bow of the kayak to the right. Place the right blade near the stern as in (A). Sweep the blade in a wide arc from the rear to front (B, C, D).

A.

B.

C.

D.

should be perpendicular or angled slightly to the surface of the water.
Sweep the paddle in a wide arc from the front of the boat to the back. Your
boat will turn sharply to the left. If the forward sweep is done on the left
side, your boat will turn to the right.

For a *reverse sweep* on the right side, put the blade in the water near
the stern of the right side of your boat. Now, sweep the paddle in a wide
arc from the back to the front. Your boat will turn sharply to the right.

Try alternating the forward and reverse sweeps on opposite sides.
For example, do a forward sweep on the right side, a reverse sweep on
the left, a forward sweep on the right, and so on. This combination will spin
the kayak around in circles to the left.

Braces

A brace stroke is handy in kayaking since it helps prevent you from
capsizing when waves or currents try to tip you over. A *simple brace* can
be done by extending your paddle at a right angle to one side of the boat.
Lean slightly to that side, as if a wave had knocked you in that direction.
Immediately after you lean, slap the water with the power face of the
blade of your paddle and push yourself upright. Lean first, then slap the
water. With this simple brace, you should be able to lean over past the
point where you would normally flip over, and upright yourself.

A more powerful type of brace is a *sweeping brace*. This brace
combines the sweeping motion that was used in the sweep strokes
described in the previous section. For a sweeping brace on the left side
place the blade in the water near the bow of the boat as you did for a
forward sweep stroke. This time the power face of the blade is held at a
thirty- to forty-five-degree angle so it planes across the top of the water.
While doing the stroke, keep the power blade on top of the water since its
surface tension helps give the paddle support.

The position that your body takes is critical. This same position
eventually will be used in the roll, and it is important to spend some time
and learn it well at the beginning. Using the left side as an example, grip
the paddle normally and hold the paddle with the blade near the bow of
the boat. The right hand, which is the upper hand gripping the paddle, is
held about six inches in front of and level with your head. The chin is
tucked in close to the left shoulder. The right arm is bent at nearly a right
angle, and the right elbow is cocked inward. The left arm is bent at nearly
or slightly greater than a right angle.

Now, sweep the paddle, keeping the power blade's face at a thirty- to
forty-five degree angle, from the front of the boat to the rear in a wide arc.
Keep the same body position throughout the sweep *by rotating your
entire upper body from the hips.* It is at this point that many people have
trouble. The motion to get the paddle around is a rotation of the body.
Everything above the waist—head, neck, shoulders, arms, and chest—
moves and keeps the same relative position throughout the sweep.
Practice it until the position and brace are comfortable.

Remember, do not use your arms to muscle the paddle around;
instead, use a rotation of the body to make the sweep. You even can
practice the body rotation in a room, by standing, gripping the paddle,
assuming the position, and twisting around as if you were making a
sweeping brace.

Try it on both sides. Choose one side that is most comfortable for you

The sweep stroke and the sweeping brace are very similar. The main difference occurs in the end result: the sweep stroke turns the kayak as shown previously; while the sweeping brace may turn the kayak some, its main function is to keep a tipping kayak from flipping upside down.

To do a sweeping brace, position your body as shown, holding the right blade of the paddle near the bow. The power face of the paddle is angled at a 30-45-degree angle to the surface of the water so it will plane across the top of the water during the stroke (*A*). Keeping the same position, sweep the paddle from the front to back by twisting the body (*B, C*). When the stroke becomes comfortable, start leaning more and more to the side you are bracing on and use the sweeping brace to upright yourself.

A.

B.

C.

and stay on this side. You eventually will use it for your rolling side. You can return later and refine the technique on the other side.

Now with your good side, start leaning a little. Lean first, then use a sweeping brace to right yourself. Have a friend stand next to the boat to flip you right side up if you happen to fall over. Since capsizing is common

Sweeping brace (*rear view*). Watch the upper arm. Keep it close to the front of the head and the elbow tucked in slightly to prevent shoulder dislocation. Here, the arm is a little high. The technique, however, is correct, with the entire body twisting around from the hips.

when you are first learning, a friend will help save you a lot of time and energy emptying the boat of water and climbing back in.

Keep working on the sweeping brace so that you can lean over and touch the side of your body to the water and still sweep yourself back up.

Bracing Hints

Here are a couple of hints that may help you on the sweeping brace:
- Be sure you fit tightly in your kayak so that the foot, knee, thigh, and hip braces (or whatever combination of braces you have) keep you from slipping around.
- You can give yourself a little mechanical advantage by slipping the upper hand (in the case of a right sweeping brace, it would be the left hand) up, next to the upper blade. The lower hand holds the paddle in the middle of the shaft. This position, sometimes called an *extended grip*, gives you a slight bit of additional power. Use the crook of the little finger of the upper hand to feel the edge of the upper blade. This "feel" can help in a whitewater situation where in the confusion of a rapid it may be difficult to tell if the paddle blade is oriented at the proper angle for a sweep.
- You also can greatly help right yourself by bringing your hips into play. As you sweep around, raise your hips up first, which turns the boat more toward an upright position. Then at the end of your stroke, bring up the rest of your body. This is the so-called *hip flick* or *hip snap* referred to in other sources. This important movement makes the uprighting process snappier. Remember, turn your hips up first, then follow with the upper body. You can get a feel for the motion by holding onto the side of the pool or holding onto the hands of a friend who is standing in the water next to you. Flip upside down. Right yourself by first bringing your hips up and then following quickly with the rest of your body. For some people, the hip flick is a tough movement to master and sometimes is best learned after the brace has been practiced extensively.

In an extended grip used during a brace or roll, the upper hand can be slipped up next to the blade. The crook of the little finger feels the blade, telling the paddler that the paddle is oriented correctly and giving him some mechanical advantage.

• If you are having trouble righting yourself after a lean, you can give yourself even more mechanical advantage by grabbing the paddle in a *Pawlata grip*. In this position the upper hand holds the *tip of the inactive blade of the paddle* while the lower hand holds the middle of the shaft. Everything else—the body position and sweeping brace motion—remains the same. By holding the paddle blade, you get a few extra feet of mechanical advantage so you can right yourself easier after a lean. Some people do not like the position, but others can have an earlier success because of the great mechanical advantage it offers. Since learning is an individualized process, choose what feels best to you.

Using the Pawlata grip in a sweeping brace gives a few extra feet of mechanical advantage.

The roll position

The Roll

To begin, first get in a roll position. I will use the right side as an example. (If your sweep felt more comfortable on the right side, the following directions will apply to you. If, however, the sweeping brace felt best on the left side, just substitute a "left" whenever "right" is used and vice versa.)

Grip your paddle normally and hold it on the left side of your kayak. This is the roll position.

Now lean to the right just a little. Do not flip upside down. Bring your paddle out of the roll position and immediately make a sweeping brace, just like you practiced previously. The idea is to feel comfortable coming out of a roll position and going directly into a sweep. The actual roll is practically the same movement.

Now let's try the real thing. Get in the roll position with the paddle to the left of the deck. Tip all the way over to the right so that you are upside down. Sit there for a moment to get oriented. You want to make the same motion of the sweeping brace, the only difference being that you are upside down. Be sure that the power face of the blade of the paddle starts on the surface of the water. A friend who is standing beside you can help put it there if you are having trouble at first. Also, be sure the power blade is at a thirty- to forty-five-degree angle to the water. As in the brace, the

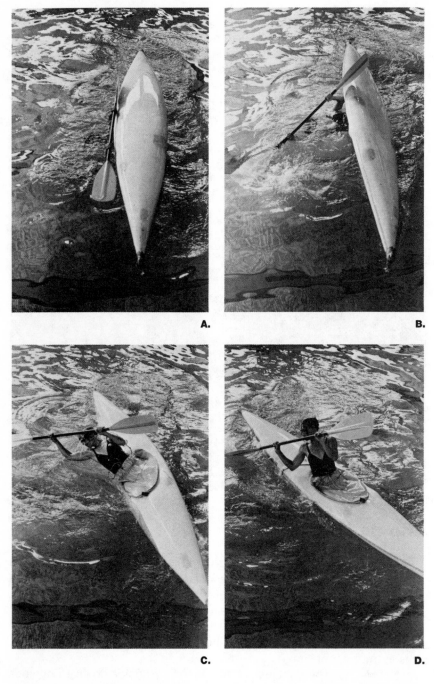

A.   B.

C.   D.

To do the roll, get into the roll position (shown in the previous photograph) and flip upside down (A). Using the same technique as the sweeping brace, sweep the paddle from the front to back by rotating the body at the hips (B, C, D). Lying far back over the rear deck of the kayak at the end of the sweep (as shown in C, or even further back than shown) will lower the center of gravity and make the roll easier.

power blade at this angle planes across the top of the water, instead of slicing through it and diving. Your friend also can help you angle it. All right, sweep your paddle.

If you get yourself up, congratulations! If not, do not worry. Learning the roll takes a lot of practice for most people. After your friend turns your kayak right side up, give it another try. If you are having problems sweeping the paddle, your friend can grab the paddle and assist you to sweep it around so you can get the feel of it.

If you are having trouble, perhaps the hints presented in the sections that follow will help.

Braces.   Since the brace and the roll are so similar, try doing several sweeping braces in a row, then immediately, without thought, get in the roll position, flip upside down, and try the roll.

Another thing you can do is keep working on the sweeping brace in lower and lower positions. Eventually, the brace can be worked to the point where you actually are tipping over so most of your body is in the water, and then bracing back up. The roll, from a position all the way upside down, will come quickly if you can brace this well.

Body Rotation.   Remember to twist or rotate the trunk of your body to make the sweeping motion of the roll.

Blade Angle.   The face of the power blade should be at a thirty- to forty-five-degree angle to the water surface. You can obtain this angle by first laying the paddle flat against the deck of your kayak and cocking or rolling your wrists to the outside. When you flip over, the power face of the blade will be in the correct position. If the blade is angled in the wrong direction, it will slice through the water, providing no support for the roll.

Life Jacket.   Wearing a life jacket will help a little when you are first learning because it will float your body up on the rolling side. When you get the roll, take off the life jacket and practice without it.

Extended Grip.   Holding your paddle in the extended grip position, as described in the previous section about bracing, will give you some mechanical advantage. Many kayakers even slip into this position on the river. It not only helps them roll, but also allows them to feel the upper blade with the little finger of the extended hand. Then they know exactly how the power face of the blade is oriented so it does not slice through the water while they are trying to roll.

Pawlata Roll.   When learning the roll, you also can give yourself greater mechanical advantage by holding the paddle in the Pawlata position, described in the bracing section. Practice a few Pawlata braces, then, keeping the same grip on the paddle, put it in the roll position. Everything—the blade angle, the body position, the rotation of the trunk —is the same as in a regular roll. The extra length of the paddle helps get you up sooner. Sometimes, after you have been trying hard for days, the Pawlata roll can give you added incentive to keep on trying. If you do learn the roll in the Pawlata position, practice it until it feels good, then immediately start working on the roll with the regular grip. This is the roll you want to strive to learn, for it is by far the best on the river.

The Pawlata roll position

Hip Flick. Payson Kennedy of the Nantahala Outdoor Center emphasizes working on the hip flick. He says (in correspondence with me):

Generally we go through a series of exercises to make this motion second nature much as you propose doing with the sweeping brace. One of the best is to have students in pairs working together in their boats. One student supports himself by holding the bow of his partner's boat which is perpendicular. He then practices overturning and righting himself while getting some support from the partner's boat. Gradually he tries to decrease the support needed, eventually going to one hand and then one finger for support. Variations can be done using the wall of a swimming pool, the hands of a partner standing on the bottom, a piece of foam or a life jacket, etc.

As an aid to assist someone in understanding what is needed in the hip flick, I tell him to use his hips and lower body to slide the boat underneath his upper body, which is supported in a horizontal position by the water and his paddle, and then push himself up off the extended paddle.

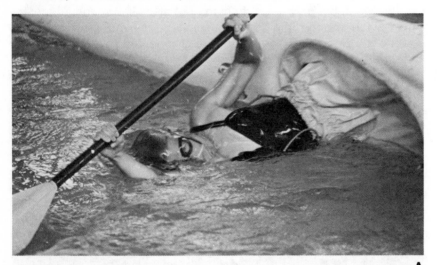

In a hip flick, the hips are raised out of the water first (A), then the upper body (B).

Head Position.   Kennedy also emphasizes head position:

Most beginners tend to lift their heads at the beginning of a roll attempt. The added weight of the head, which must be supported by the paddle, makes it difficult to complete the roll successfully. Instead, keep the head tucked against the right shoulder for a roll on the right and supported by the water until the roll is almost complete. Then bring it up last when the boat is sliding underneath the body to support the extra weight.

Other Hints.   Dick Held of Whitewater Boats (Cedar City, Utah) suggests using a mask to watch your paddle sweep. In this way, your body rotates with the paddle. Pete Skinner of the American Whitewater Affiliation (West Sand Lake, New York) and Rob Lesser, also of the AWA and a well-known kayaker, believe the key to an effective roll is to lie back over the rear deck of the boat at the end of the sweep. By lying back, your center of gravity is close to the boat and the boat turns into an upright position more easily. For this reason, Skinner and Lesser feel that kayaks should be constructed with low rear decks.

Preventing Shoulder Dislocation

One last note about braces and rolls: When you are learning, get in the habit of keeping the upper arm's elbow in tight and close to your chest. If your elbow is held out or if the upper arm is extended above your head, the shoulder becomes very vulnerable to dislocation, one of the most common of kayaking injuries. It has happened to me twice, but the trick of keeping the elbow in has helped immensely.

Another help in preventing shoulder dislocation is to rotate the body when bracing or making strokes. "If the body is rotated," Kennedy says, "so that the arm is never extended behind the shoulder, the chance of a dislocation is reduced and the power of the stroke is increased."

Ferrying Techniques

A basic move that you will want to learn as soon as you get on moving water is the ferry. It is a way of moving from one side of the river to the other without drifting (or with very little drifting) down the river. There are two types, the upstream ferry and the back ferry.

Upstream Ferry.   In this ferry you point the boat upstream and paddle forward. Adjust the forward paddling so that it equals the current and you stay in the same spot on the river. Now angle your boat toward the opposite shore and keep paddling. The angle will enable you to move over to the opposite shore.

While crossing a river, the current sometimes will be strong and other times will be weak. With faster water, you will have to maintain a slight angle upstream to cancel out the stronger current. With slower currents you can hold a greater angle or ease up on the forward paddling. As you ferry across the river, feel the current and adjust the angle of your boat and/or paddling speed correspondingly.

One of the greatest changes from slower to faster water is when you ferry from the slow-moving water on the side of the river (or out from any

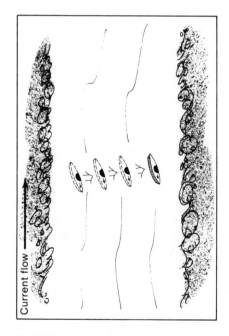

Upstream ferry in a kayak (*top view*). With the boat faced upstream against the current, the kayaker paddles forward, gradually angling the boat toward the opposite shore and leaning downstream (to the boatman's left here) as he ferries across.

eddy) into the main current. The fast-moving current tends to spin the boat downstream. To maintain the ferry position with your bow pointing upstream, paddle hard on the side of the boat turning downstream, or rudder your paddle a little near the stern of the boat on the upstream side.

A very important aspect of ferrying is to keep a downstream lean while angling across. The stronger the current, the more the lean. The reason is that if you lean upstream, the onrushing water will hit the deck of your boat, pushing it under and possibly capsizing the boat. Upstream leans are one of the most common causes of flips. Get in the habit of leaning whenever ferrying.

Back Ferry.   Back ferrying is similar to the upstream ferrying, except that you face downstream and back paddle against the current. Angle the back end of your boat to the opposite shore and ferry over. The same downstream lean applies on the back ferry as in the upstream ferry.

Comparison of Ferrying Techniques.   The strongest method is the upstream ferry since the powerful forward stroke comes into play. It is used extensively by kayakers. The back ferry is not so strong, but it does have the advantage of keeping you faced downstream so you can see what is coming at all times. It is handy in tight spots where there is no time to turn around to get into an upstream ferry position. The back ferry is particularly useful in small, shallow rocky streams with tight passageways and numerous rocks.

Bends

If you know that the outside of a corner or a bend is clear of obstacles, you may wish to take the fastest run, which is on the outside. However, if you are not sure of the outside, or know that it harbors overhanging trees or other obstacles, stay on the inside.

There are two ways to stay to the inside. One is to back paddle, pointing the back end of the boat to the inside of the bend and backing around it. As you have learned in the ferry, try to feel the current and adjust your boat angle so that you paddle against the currents that may try to sweep your boat to the outside.

Or you can point the nose of your boat to the inside of the corner and paddle forward against the current.

Either method works fine. The bow to the inside is the strongest and puts you in a good position to pull off in any available eddies if the going looks too rough as you round the corner.

Eddies

Eddies created behind rocks give the kayaker a great deal of freedom to maneuver through rapids. The basic technique utilizing eddies is the *eddy turn*.

A simple eddy turn is made by paddling toward an eddy behind a rock. When you are first learning, start with a large rock since the eddy will be larger there. Enter just behind the rock, where the eddy is strongest. Stroke hard to drive the boat across the eddy line. Once the bow of the boat breaks through the line and glides into the eddy, the boat will pivot quickly, turning you upstream. Because of the pivot, you must lean to the inside to counteract the centrifugal force, which can knock you over to

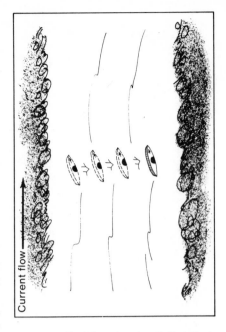

Back ferry in a kayak (*top view*). The boat is faced downstream and the kayaker back paddles against the current flow as he angles the back of the boat toward the opposite shore. The kayaker maintains a downstream lean (to the boatman's right here) while ferrying.

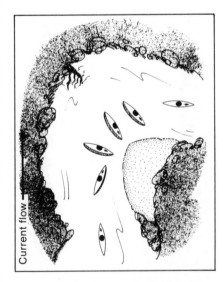

When moving around a sharp bend (*top view*), stay to the inside by pointing the bow of the kayak toward the inside of the bend and keep paddling to stay in close. (This maneuver also can be done by pointing the stern to the inside and back paddling.)

the outside.

To help support the lean, hold the paddle in a *high brace* position on the inside of the pivot. The high brace is similar to the sweeping brace except that the paddle is held stationary out to the side of the boat and is not swept. For example, to do a high brace on the right side, grip the paddle normally. The left hand is several inches in front of the head, the left elbow is cocked inward, and the right arm is bent at just slightly greater than a right angle. The paddle extends straight out from the side of the boat, with the power face of the blade flat against the water surface.

Let's put it all together in an example. You are floating downstream and see an eddy to your right that you want to turn into. Turn your boat toward the eddy and paddle toward it. Enter just behind the rock and cross the eddy line with good hard strokes. As soon as you feel the boat begin to pivot, lean on a high brace on your right side, which is the inside of the pivot. Voilà! You are in the eddy and can go back to an upright position.

Eddy turn (*top view*). The kayaker sees the eddy (*A*) and paddles toward the top of it (*B*). When the kayak crosses the eddy line and begins to pivot, the kayaker leans and does a high brace on the inside of the pivot (*C*). After the kayak pivots in the eddy, the kayaker regains his upright position (*D*).

Other strokes can be used when turning into eddies. Just before entering an eddy, you can help swing the boat in with a strong sweep stroke on the outside. As soon as the boat begins to turn in, lean on a high brace on the inside of the pivot to balance yourself.

A method of snapping the boat into the eddy is a technique called the *Duffek*. As an example, to turn the boat into an eddy located on your right side, begin by making one sweep stroke on the left or outside of the turn, as mentioned in the previous paragraph. The sweep will begin to turn you into the eddy. Now reach out on your right side, placing the right blade of the paddle in the slow- or upstream-moving water of the eddy. The position you assume as you reach out is exactly the same as the high brace except for one important difference: the position of the blade. In the Duffek, roll your wrists back and face the power face of the blade forward. In other words, the power face of the blade, which usually faces toward the stern, now faces toward the bow. By holding the right blade in this position for a moment and then drawing the blade toward the bow as in a bow draw, the kayak literally will snap behind the eddy. If you desire, you can turn the paddle blade that is now near the bow of the boat so that the power face is facing toward the stern in a normal position, and then make a forward stroke to help maintain your position behind the eddy.

The upper arm position in the high brace, and particularly in the Duffek stroke, makes the shoulder vulnerable to dislocation. Use caution with the Duffek, and stick to easy eddies when possible. For high water conditions with strong eddies, the high brace is safer. Yet when making the high brace, be sure to keep the elbow of the upper arm cocked inward.

Eddy Turn Hints.   When doing eddy turns, use hard strokes to cross the eddy line. Enter the eddy near the top to take advantage of the stronger currents. (Occasionally, a kayaker's bow will hit the rock while doing an eddy turn, and it is a good idea to tape a split tennis ball or other padding to the nose to protect it.)

Lean to the inside when you feel the eddy pivoting you around upstream. Use a high brace to help support your lean to the inside. Keep the elbow of the upper arm cocked in to prevent a dislocation. After you have spun into the eddy, the support of the brace ends and you go back to an upright position.

Turning out of Eddies.   To get out of an eddy, you can let your boat drift downstream and back out. However, it is more effective to do what sometimes is termed the "*peel off*." To describe the "peel off," let's examine coming out of an eddy on the right side. Position yourself several feet behind the rock forming the eddy, then paddle hard forward, breaking through near the top of the eddy line at about a forty-five-degree angle. When the boat hits the downstream current, the boat will spin downstream. Counteract this by leaning toward the right on a downstream high brace.

Current flow ⟶

When turning out of an eddy, the paddle is in a high brace position as the boat pivots around to point downstream.

Use of Eddies.   Turning into an eddy gives you a chance to stop, look around, and decide on a route. Eddies on the side of the river offer a place for you to stop, get out, and scout. Whenever running a river, always keep a mental note where eddies are located. While in a rapid, look ahead and pick out eddies that you can pull into and stop. If for some reason something in a rapid ahead demands a more careful look, you will know exactly where the stopping places are located.

Eddies can help you move from one side to another. You can turn into an eddy on one side and break in the current on the other to put you in the location you need to be to run the rapid.

Kayaker in eddy (*top view*)

Holes

Small holes that are not symmetrical can be run any way: forward, backward, or sideways. When running through a small hole, lean into the curling, foamy wave using a high brace. Then reach over the curling-back wave and catch the downriver current and pull yourself through. Be sure to lean into the wave; the more forceful the wave is slapping upstream, the more you will have to lean. If you lean away from the hole, the combination of the curling-back wave and the downstream current hitting the deck of your kayak quickly will capsize your boat in the upstream direction.

Bigger, meaner holes usually are avoided by most kayakers. If you run into one by accident or on purpose, turn the boat so that you run through the hole faced downstream and paddle, stroking as quickly and as hard as possible, to gain enough momentum to push through it.

Standing Waves

Standing waves or haystacks can be run sideways, forward, or backward. As with holes, it is important to lean downstream if you run through standing waves sideways. Many boaters run straight on and paddle through large standing waves that are crashing back forming a

Current flow ———————▶

The lean is an all-important technique of kayaking. Without a paddle, the kayaker here is able to keep himself upright by leaning as he rides a small hole sideways.

Leaning into a hole

hole.

Symmetrical standing waves can be used for *surfing*. Commonly, standing waves form at the end of a rapid or after a constriction in the river. Ideally, it is nice to have an eddy on one side from which the kayaker can do an upstream ferry into the wave. The wave is entered so that the kayak slips into the upstream face of the wave. On the right wave, gravity pulls the kayak down, but the downstream rushing current balances the force of gravity and holds the kayak in place.

If it feels as if the kayak is drifting away, paddle hard forward to keep it on the face of the wave. The bow may be pushed off in either direction and you will have to respond quickly by ruddering your paddle near the stern of the boat. Remember to lean downstream if your kayak angles in either direction. If you do not, the onrushing water may catch your deck and capsize the boat upstream. Lean as you make the ruddering motions. In order to keep the kayak facing upstream, it sometimes may be necessary to lean in one direction and rudder on the opposite side.

To slide into surfing waves, the paddle is ruddered near the stern of the boat. When the boat is angled, a downstream lean is maintained. If the bow is pushed off in one direction, the paddler counters by ruddering on the upstream side.

On long, symmetrical waves you may be able to surf back and forth from one end of the wave to the other.

Besides being fun, surfing can be helpful in running rapids. Catching a surf from an upstream ferry, a kayaker can glide from one side of the river to the other to get in position to run a part of a rapid. Often it is handy to use surfing to move from one eddy to another. Paddle out from the eddy, but instead of turning downstream as with the peel off, keep the boat pointed upstream. Catch a surf if suitable waves exist, and glide over to the next eddy.

Big Water

Big water is the condition on some rivers during high water or on other rivers anytime of the year when waves and holes are big and violent. One of the earliest advocates of a big water technique was the late Walt Blackadar, a famous kayaker from Idaho. In 1971 in the winter issue of the *American Whitewater Journal*, he first wrote of a style of boating with personal adaptations that has since gained wide acceptance: running sideways down a river. When a boater comes to the top of large standing waves, he leans downstream to prevent upstream flips. If the wave curls back, he reaches downstream in a high brace position (watching the upper arm so it does not get too high) and leans downstream, which will wash the boat through the wave right side up.

Blackadar claimed that the conventional style of riding down a river with the bow pointed downstream and paddling forward through big waves only increases the boater's speed and he loses valuable time to make decisions and moves in the rapid. In the Blackadar strategy, the boater avoids big holes or rocks in the sideways position simply by making a few strokes backward or forward to carry him around the holes or rocks. Blackadar even claimed that running backward with the bow pointed upstream was a prefectly valid technique in big water. From the reverse position a boater can brace over either shoulder and execute the strong upstream ferry to move around any bad holes.

For shallow, rocky rapids, alignment of the bow downstream is important to prevent broaching (see the "Safety" chapter). But the beauty of the Blackadar style is that it is not necessarily a style reserved only for big violent water. It can be utilized by recreational boaters in many other rapids or parts of rapids where the rocks are not too numerous to prevent the boater from running sideways.

Pop-ups and "Endos"

It is possible to surf on a hole that is safe and will not hold you. You can surf sideways in a hole or you can surf in the regular method, with the bow of your kayak pointing upstream. When you surf some holes with the bow pointing upstream, a strong diving current may force the bow downward under the water. If it is pushed down deep enough, the back end of the kayak will pop into the air. This is called a *pop-up*. If the bow is carried downstream while under the water, the kayak may flip end over end. This, one of the most dramatic tricks in kayaking, is called an "*endo*" or "*ender*." Some kayakers can back into a hole and do a back "*endo*." Whenever attempting "*endos*" and pop-ups, be sure to use foam walls. The water pounding on your deck can split seams and crack decks.

Running a Rapid

Looking at the illustration of a possible rapid that a kayaker might run, let's see how he might use these various techniques to run it.

The entrance to this rapid is marked with two downstream Vs. The first V (A) leads into a large hole (C), and the kayaker decides not to run that one. The second V (B) is clean, so he enters there. But soon after entering, he has to make a move away from the large boulders (D) on the right side of the river farther down. He does an eddy turn behind one boulder (E). From there he turns out of the eddy, keeping his nose upstream, and does an upstream ferry or surfs to behind the eddy behind another boulder (F). He turns out of the eddy and heads down the river, nose first, missing some large holes (G), but runs through some smaller holes (H). A tree (I) overhangs the outside of the bend, so the kayaker points his bow toward the inside of the bend and paddles to stay close to the right shore. The rapid is successfully run; he gives a cheer and waits for all his companions to make it safely through.

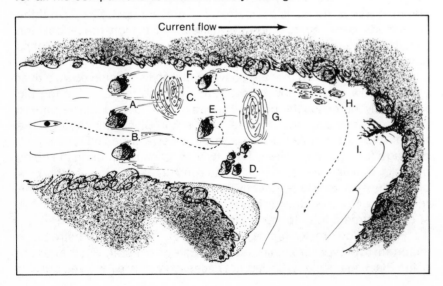

Running a rapid in a kayak (*top view*). Downstream Vs (*A*, *B*), large hole (*C*), large boulders (*D*), another single boulder (*E*), another boulder (*F*), large holes (*G*), smaller holes (*H*), tree (*I*).

A pop-up

RAFT TECHNIQUE

The small inflatable raft banged into another rock, jerking me from my position on the side tube. I leaped back on the tube and paddled furiously with my two companions, Harrison Hilbert, whom everyone affectionately calls "H," and John Merriam.

At the mercy of the current, we rushed toward another rock and collided again. But this time the boat did not bounce; it stuck fast and became broached. Had we known better, we would have shifted our weight to the downstream tube against the rock. But knowing little about white water, I instead stayed on the upstream tube, flailing with my paddle. John climbed up on the rock and the side that H was on immediately was sucked under the rushing current. H, finding himself rapidly sinking deeper and deeper in water, had enough of the raft and jumped into the rapid.

Then the boat surged and slid off the rock. With water sloshing up to our knees, John and I chased H down the river. He swam ahead of us, holding his paddle in the air and pushing off rocks. John and I followed, spinning in circles, jerking, careening, and banging off rocks. Finally we reached H and dragged him into the boat, then continued bouncing and banging down the river.

It was a shaky start for us, but we gradually began to read the water better. We avoided any more close encounters with rocks and refined our paddling so our route through rapids was not a series of uncontrollable spins. We began to work as a team, and with each successful run we cheered, and around campfires at night, we joked of the mistakes and talked proudly of the successful runs.

The sharing of successes and mistakes with the other members of your boat is one of the most rewarding aspects of running a paddle boat. Moreover, unlike John, H, and me at the beginning of our trip, a well-practiced paddling crew, especially in smaller technical rivers, can be highly effective.

This chapter will deal with both paddle and oar boat techniques.

Paddle Rafts

In many ways the maneuvers made by a paddle boat and a kayak are very similar. To understand the basics of paddle raft technique, be sure to read the "Kayak Technique" chapter, particularly the information about ferrying techniques, bends, eddies, and holes. If you find yourself becoming an aficionado of paddle boats—and paddle rafting can be addicting—you will want to read the excellent chapter on paddle rafting prepared by Payson Kennedy in *The All-Purpose Guide to Paddling* (see the "Books" section in the "Sources" chapter). In the following sections we will look at some of the basic concepts and techniques pertaining particularly to paddle boats.

Leadership of the Raft.   The disadvantage of a paddle boat is that messages about maneuvers must be relayed to, and put into action by, the rest of the members of the raft. To make this process efficient, one member of the paddle crew should be selected as the "captain." When in a rapid, he should be the only person to make calls. Any other chiefs will serve only to add confusion and indecision when quick reaction time is necessary. Switch captains so everyone has the chance to be the leader of the boat. The more one particular group works together, the more efficient and skillful it will become.

Bracing and Positioning of Paddlers.   Different paddlers use different positions to anchor themselves in the boat. One of the best methods is that advocated by Payson Kennedy of the Nantahala Outdoor Center (Bryson City, North Carolina). He recommends that each paddler lean with his hip against the *inside* of the tube and stretch one leg midway or all the way across the raft to brace against and under the cross tube or thwart to achieve a secure position. Kennedy adds (in correspondence with me):

Stretching a leg across a boat is one way of bracing in a paddle boat. A better, safer position is to stretch a leg midway under a cross tube.

> The heel of the extended leg is against and protected by the cross tube. The heel of the extended leg is actually pushed back a bit under the curvature of the cross tube so that the paddler can hold himself in the raft if he starts to bounce out. On harder rivers now we are mostly using rafts with three cross tubes and six paddlers. Everyone is able to sit in the corner of a cross tube and side tube (except stern paddlers), the leg is extended less than to the middle of the raft, and the toes are secured under the cross tube ahead.

Taller rafters may be able to stretch one leg all the way across the raft to brace their foot against the other tube, but it is important that paddlers are careful to avoid injury by quickly moving their legs out of the way if someone in the boat is thrown out of position. In rocky rivers, this method is preferable to sitting directly on top of the tube, with one leg on the inside and one leg dangling in the water on the other side. The outside leg in this so-called "cowboy style" is vulnerable to injury if the boat is swept against rocks. On larger rivers where rocks are not a problem, however, the cowboy position is frequently utilized. In the easy water between rapids, paddlers can take any position that is comfortable, including the cowboy position.

Try to arrange paddlers so that you have about equal power on each side of the boat. If you ever are knocked down on the floor in any inflatable raft, get off the floor immediately or injury may occur if the boat bangs over rocks.

Basic Moves.   To turn the boat, paddlers on one side paddle forward while those on the other side back paddle. For instance, to turn the front end of the boat to the right, paddlers on the right side back paddle, while paddlers on the left paddle forward.

The "cowboy style" of bracing in a paddle raft

Draw stroke (*side view*) can be used to move a paddle raft a slight distance sideways. To move to the right, paddlers on the right execute draw strokes. Paddlers on left pry the paddle through the water away from the boat or execute forward sweeps. A raft moving sideways encounters great resistance and this technique is used only once in a while when slight adjustments are necessary to avoid obstructions.

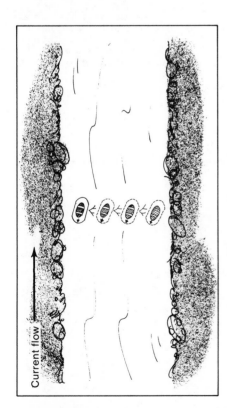

Upstream ferry in a paddle raft (*top view*). The front end of the boat is headed upstream and angled to the left side of the river (or the paddlers' right, viewed from their upstream position) as the boaters paddle forward.

If the boat needs to be moved a short distance sideways, a *draw stroke* can be used. For instance, to move it to the right, paddlers on the right side reach out to the side with their paddles and draw them strongly until they are next to the boat. The paddlers on the right continue making draw strokes until the boat reaches the desired position. Les Bechdel of the Nantahala Outdoor Center recommends that paddlers on the left side do forward sweeps (see the "Sweep Strokes" section in the "Kayak Technique" chapter). This method is used to make slight adjustments to either side. It is not powerful enough when distances over a few feet must be traveled.

Ferry. This maneuver, as described in the "Kayak Technique" chapter, can be done as either an upstream or a back ferry. In the *upstream ferry*, the raft is faced upstream while everyone paddles forward, angling the raft to the right or left toward the bank to which they are ferrying. From the upstream ferry position, paddlers must look over their shoulders to see what is coming up on the river, but it is the most powerful of the ferry moves. In the *back ferry*, the boat is faced downstream and everyone back paddles, angling the back end of the raft to the right or left toward the bank to which they are heading. This technique gives the occupants a better view, but a slightly weaker ferry. It is useful for making moves around rocks, when the river channel is too tight to use the methods described next.

Rocks. To maneuver around a rock, the paddle boat is turned before approaching the rock too closely, either to the right or left, depending on which side the captain chooses. Everyone paddles forward, moving the boat to one side of the rock. When the boat is clear of the rock, the boat is straightened again. For a more efficient turn in tight spots, Kennedy suggests (in his chapter in *The All-Purpose Guide to Paddling*) using a combination of strokes. Let's say you have just come through a chute and must make a quick move to the right of a boulder sticking out. To do so, the right bow paddler executes a series of draw strokes. Meanwhile, the right stern paddler executes a reverse quarter sweep. The left side does either forward strokes or forward sweeps. This technique, as Kennedy notes, helps move the boat to the right during the turn. The usual method of forward paddling on one side and back paddling on the other, turns the boat, but while the turning takes place, the boat continues to be swept by the current toward the rock. The use of sweeps and draws helps prevent this.

Eddies. Eddies are utilized much like they are in kayaking. The boat is pointed toward the eddy, everyone paddles hard to cross the eddy line, and the boat pivots behind the rock. If an eddy is not large enough to stop the boat, it can be used to slow down the boat's progress slightly and to assist the paddle crew in moving from one side to another.

Holes. Big holes are best avoided. If a hole must be run, the paddle crew should hit it straight, paddling hard to break through. Once the front paddlers are through the curling-back wave, they should continue to paddle hard so that the boat is not pulled back in the hole. If the boat begins the turn sideways, the crew should be ready to make any adjustments to straighten it out quickly. When a boat is sideways in a hole it is very vulnerable to flipping.

Weight Shifts. Weight can be shifted in paddle boats, making them a versatile craft. For turning into a strong eddy, the paddlers should shift their weight to the upstream side; for turning out of an eddy, they should shift to the downstream side. In both cases, the weight shift prevents onrushing water from spilling over the tubes and into the boat. If a boat turns sideways in a hole, all weight should be shifted to the downstream side to prevent the upstream tube from diving and the downstream tube from being thrown upward, capsizing the boat. While leaning on the downstream tube, the paddlers can reach out over the top of the curling-back wave in a high brace position similar to the one used in kayaking as an additional measure for preventing the boat from flipping.

Oar Rafts

One of the most skillful runs I have ever watched of a small oar boat in big water was performed by Tolly Tollefson in the granddaddy of Colorado River rapids, Lava Falls. Don, her companion in the boat, shoved her off and sat in the front seat of the small twelve-foot boat. She hovered above the rapid, ferrying back and forth to adjust her position above the entrance, which dropped into two huge waves that came together and formed a furious V.

She accelerated down the smooth water, pushing on her oars to gain speed, and then hit the middle of the V. The boat reared up and Don jumped on the side tube to bring it back down. They disappeared for a moment in the foam, then reappeared, speeding for the large block of basalt on the right. Tolly pulled madly several times to pull away. There was not much she could do in the powerful current, but it was enough to set her up so she squarely hit the waves crashing down from above. Again the boat tipped to one side, but Don jumped on the high end, grabbing gear bags to keep himself from being washed out and brought the boat down. They were home free when they hit the large standing waves at the bottom of the rapid.

The remaining sections in this chapter describe the basic maneuvers and techniques of running an oar raft.

Basic Maneuvers in an Oar Raft. Tolly's maneuvers in Lava Falls can be traced to several basic moves. At the top of the rapid she *pushed* on the oars to help propel her through the big holes at the top. Pushing the oars also can be used on quieter stretches to help speed up your progress while floating down the river. The pushing motion keeps you facing downstream so you can see everything that is coming. For easy moves around rocks where the current is not too swift, you easily can push the boat around.

In the midst of Lava, in her attempt to move away from the block of basalt, Tolly *pulled* on the oars. Pulling is your strongest stroke on the oars since you can throw your whole body into the pull. Pulling also slows the boat down a tad to help give you more time.

For *turning* the boat, think in terms of the rear of the raft. If you pull on the right oar, the back end will turn toward the left shore. If you pull on the left, the back end will turn toward the right. Pulling on an oar will turn you, but the quickest and most powerful turn is to pull on one oar and push on the other; in other words, pulling on the right oar and at the same time pushing on the left pivots the back end to the left. In a rapid, you want to use this way of pivoting the boat as much as possible.

Ferry. To ferry an oar raft from one side of the river to the other, face the boat downstream as you normally would in the oaring position and pull on the oars. Pull enough to equalize the force of the current so you stay in one spot on the river. Then angle your back end slightly toward

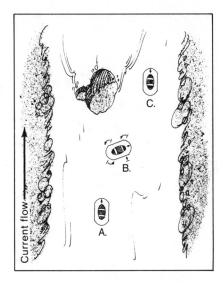

Paddle raft moving around a rock (*top view*). The paddlers spot the rock (*A*). To turn the raft to the right and minimize drift toward the rock, the right bow paddler executes draw strokes. The right stern paddler executes a reverse sweep. Paddlers on left execute forward strokes or forward sweep strokes (*B*). When the raft is turned to the right, all boatmen paddle forward until raft is clear of the rock (*C*). When clear, the paddlers straighten the raft and continue down the river.

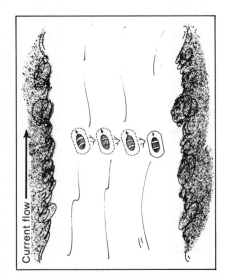

Ferrying in an oar raft (*top view*). The boat is faced downstream as the oarsman pulls on the oars, angling the stern to the right side of the river.

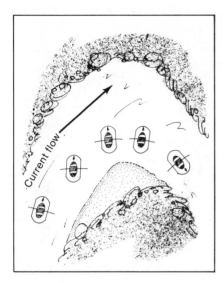

Moving around a bend in an oar raft (*top view*). The raft enters the bend on the inside, pointing its back end toward the inside.

Oar raft moving around a sharp bend. The back end is pointed toward the inside of the bend as the oarsman comes around. (Current is flowing toward foreground.)

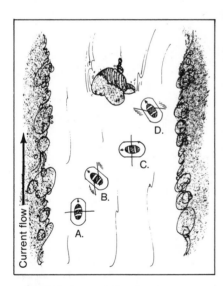

Moving around a rock in an oar raft (*top view*). The oarsman spots the rock and decides to run it to the right (*A*). He pivots the raft so its back end is facing right (*B*). He then pulls on the oars to move the raft to the right (*C*). Once past the rock, he pivots the raft so it is facing downstream again (*D*).

the opposite shore. By pulling on the oars you gradually will work your way over to the other side.

The current as you cross a river will vary from weak sections to more powerful areas. In weaker currents, angle your boat more toward the opposite shore. In stronger currents, angle less. Keep aware of the strength of the current and adjust the angle accordingly.

Ferrying is used extensively by oar rafters to move the raft and to position it in rapids. You can use it to move over to the other side of the river if a better channel exists there, move around rocks, or jockey for position before entering a drop.

Bends.   If the outside of a bend looks clean, you may want to stay on the outside to follow the fastest current. If you are not sure what is around the bend, it is best to enter near the inside. As you work your way around, keep the back end of the boat pointed toward the inside and keep pulling on the oars so the boat remains on the inside.

Rocks above the Water Surface.   There are three ways of moving around rocks depending on the situation. If the current is not swift, you can *push* on the oars to go around either side of the rock, then turn straight and continue down the river.

If the current is swift or you are in the midst of a rapid, you will want to move around a rock by *pulling* on the oars. If you look ahead and decide

to go around the right side of the rock, turn the *back end* of the boat to the right. Pull on the oars so that the raft moves right. Turn the raft straight, and continue down the river.

The quickest way to move the raft to the side is to turn the boat so that the back end is at a ninety-degree angle to the riverbank, and pull on the oars to move. If there are big waves or holes in the rapid, you may not want to maintain this extreme perpendicular angle since the boat can take in too much water or flip if the hole is a thrasher. In this case you may keep the boat at an angle that is less than perpendicular and *ferry* across. By ferrying, your forward progress down the river is slowed down as you move to the side, giving you additional time to look ahead and make decisions.

If in getting around a rock, you find that you may not have time to turn the boat, pull away from the rock, and turn the boat back downstream again, you can use a third technique. Let's say you rapidly are approaching several boulders blocking the left side of the river. You pivot your boat quickly, and pull on the oars hard to the right trying to miss the rocks. If you have little distance left between you and one of the rocks, pivoting the front end of the boat back downstream, as in a normal method of moving around a rock, may cause you to lose momentum to the right, and hit the rock. Instead, pivot around backward by pulling hard on the left oar (see the back pivot illustration). The right oar next to the rock will be in the way if the turn is tight and you will have to get it out of the way by *shipping* it as explained in the next section. This maneuver, called the *back pivot* by some boaters, is used only in tight spots. It leaves your boat in a position of running backward down the river. When it is safe to do so, you will want to pivot the boat back around.

Shipping the Oars.   When executing the back pivot, as mentioned in the preceding section, or when running close to rocks, you may need to get one or both of your oars out of the way. There are two ways of doing it. If you look ahead and know in advance that you need to get one or more oars out of the way, you can *ship forward* by tucking the oar blades in close to the front part of the boat. To do it, pull your arms in and rotate your hands down. As soon as you pass the obstacle, you can put the oars back in place.

If you have misjudged and suddenly are sliding by very close to a rock, you can get your oar out of the way by pushing it forward until the oar blade has cleared the rock. This technique, called *shipping backward*, leaves you off-balance and is not so smooth and effective as shipping the oar forward.

Hitting Rocks and Cliffs.   If you find yourself heading for a rock, pull as hard as you can to try to avoid the serious situation of washing broadside against it. If you make it to the edge of the rock, you may be able to catch the water spilling off the side, and you can wash around the obstacle by going into a back pivot. If not, try to hit the rock dead on with the nose of the boat. Use the same method on a cliff. If the water washes you into a cliff, hit it with the nose of your boat and pull away. If you hit the cliff sideways, you will lose the use of one of the oars and your ability to pull away.

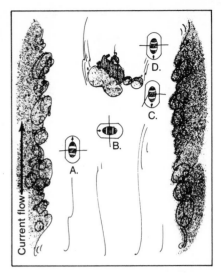

Back pivot in an oar raft (*top view*). The oarsman spots a rock that must be run on the right (*A*). He pivots the raft so its stern faces right (*B*). He just barely clears the rock and does not have room to turn to a normal downstream position, so he turns the back end downriver, shipping the oar that is close to the rock out of the way (*C*). He keeps the raft in a backward position until it is safe to pivot the front end around (*D*).

Shipping oar forward

To clear the rock, the oarsman first starts pulling to the right. He fights a strong current and is not quite able to make the pull. With the bow of the raft, he hits the rock and the current spins the boat backward and safely past the rock. In any type of raft, the boat never should be allowed to wash broadside against a rock. (Opposite page)

If you do wash into a rock sideways, the boat may bounce a little. Time the bounce and direction of the bounce, and with quick reactions you may be able to spin the boat off the rock. For information on what to do if the boat is pinned broadside on the rock, see the chapter about hazards.

Shallow Rocks. Rocks hidden just under the water can hang up a boat. You may be able to spin the boat off as soon as you feel the floor scraping across the rock. If the raft catches and becomes hung up, you may be able to shift the passengers' weight in the boat to the side away from the rock and bounce from side to side to get the boat off. Or if the water is shallow enough, you may have to jump out and push the boat off the rock. Be careful whenever you are in the river. At all costs, avoid getting a foot caught between submerged rocks.

Eddies. For an oar boat to be able to stop behind an eddy as a kayak can, the eddy must be good-sized. More often, eddies are useful to help an oarsman move from one side of the river to the other. For example, let's say you want to move from the left to the right and on the planned pathway an eddy is located behind a rock. Start ferrying to the right. Pull hard when you reach the eddy behind the rock (trying to get an

If a raft gets hung up on shallow rocks, try shifting the weight of passengers to one side, or bouncing the raft, or it may be necessary to get out and push.

To ferry from the right to the left side of the photo, the oarsman uses the eddy behind the rock.

oar in the eddy will help). The eddy will slow you down and if you are close enough behind the rock, the eddy current often will give the raft an extra push to the right. This little boost may be just enough for you to gain the position you need.

Stopping.   If the current is not strong, stopping is just a matter of pulling off to the side of the river and jumping out with the stern line. If the current is swift or the river is high, you will want to use a more careful procedure. Look for large eddies where you can stop on the side of the river. Eddies that are large enough for the boat may not always be available, but even a small one can help. One of the passengers should be behind the oarsman in the back of the boat, holding the stern line and ready to go. The oarsman ferries to the side of the river. As he gets close to shore and while he still has room to pull on the oar closest to the shore, he slows the boat as much as he possibly can. Then he points the back end into whatever eddy is available and pulls into shore. With the one oar still available, he tries to slow the boat so the person in the back can get out with the line and hold the boat in place.

The stern line always should be available in the rear of the boat. To coil the line, use the method described in the chapter about hazards, or better yet, use a throw bag (also described in that chapter) to hold the line. Some people even make an open bag out of raft material, and glue it to the tube of the raft in the stern to provide a convenient place to store both the stern and bow lines and keep them out of the way. The free end of the line should be coiled or put in the bag first, while the end attached to the boat should be the last loops on the coil or the last of the line in the throw bag. The person holding the rope *picks up the end of the line attached to the boat* and lets it slide through his hand so that a constant tension can be maintained on the boat. If the other end—the free end—of the rope is picked up first, the boat may float down the river and gain momentum before he has a chance to stop it.

Moving from Slow to Fast Water.   If you are in an eddy or in any situation where you are moving from an area of slow water to fast downstream current, pull hard on the oars to break into the faster current. Enter the faster moving current at a forty-five-degree angle. When the boat enters the fast current, it will tend to be spun backward downstream. To prevent this, keep pulling on the downstream oar. The stream of very fast water may even push the upstream tube under the water; on small boats, you can negate the effect by having passengers shift their weight to the downstream tube.

Holes.   Small holes where there is no danger of scraping the boat or flipping can be used to slow the boat a little to give yourself more time to make a move. Larger holes usually are avoided.

If you are forced or pushed into a good-sized hole, turn the boat straight so you will hit the hole as squarely as possible. If you have time, push hard on the oar before dropping in the hole. Try to create some momentum in order to break through. As you hit the curling-back wave, get ready with your oars to pivot the boat if the hole knocks you to one side. At all costs avoid getting swept sideways in the hole, which will make the boat very vulnerable to slipping.

If the boat does turn sideways, passengers can help by quickly shifting their weight to the downstream side. Especially in smaller boats, the downstream weight may be enough to prevent the boat from flipping.

Some boaters, when running extremely big water with holes impossible to miss, purposely will bail water into the boat before starting or will

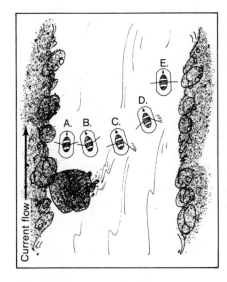

Moving from slow to fast water in an oar raft (*top view*). The raft is in an eddy with the *back end* facing upstream (*A*). The oarsman points the back end into the fast-moving current and pulls hard on the oars (*B*). As the raft hits the faster current, the oarsman pulls hard on the right oar and holds the left oar stationary in the water (*C*). When the raft is well into the fast water (*D*), then he pivots into a normal downstream position (*E*).

drop through a smaller hole sideways to take on water. A boat full of water can crash through big holes that would flip dry craft, but the filled boat also is heavy and extremely difficult to maneuver.

Standing Waves.   Standing waves are run straight on. If you want to minimize the amount of water that is splashed into the boat, you can angle the boat slightly off to one side and pull on the oars a little while rising up over the waves.

It is possible to use a standing wave to assist you in moving from one side of the river to the other. By ferrying hard before reaching the upstream face of the wave, the boat can catch just a slight surf, which is similar to the surfing maneuver done by kayakers. This slight surf can help move you across to the desired location.

Additional Oar Boat Hints.   Try to make your strokes with the oar quick and shallow. Shallow oaring is especially helpful when you are moving sideways. A deep downstream oar can hit underwater rocks and be pulled under as the boat rolls over it. A deep oar stroke also can be hard to control when side and swirling currents catch the oar.

In a raft, you have the advantage of being able to stand up and get a better view of the rapid in front of you. After you have had a look, sit down and get ready for the ride.

Remember to use opposite motions on the oars when you pivot—pushing on one oar and pulling on the other. Try to make pivots on the crests of waves. As the boat rises up, there is less friction on it and it is easier to move. In wave troughs, it is more difficult to move.

When running a hole, the oarsman keeps the boat straight and pushes through.

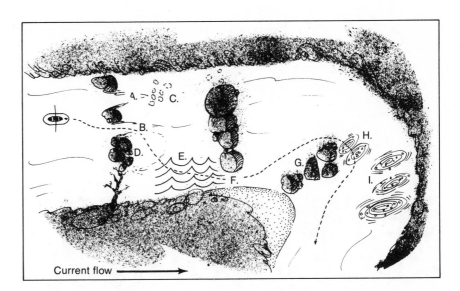

Running a rapid in an oar raft (*top view*). Downstream Vs (*A*, *B*), shallow rocks (*C*), eddy (*D*), large waves (*E*), rock (*F*), boulders (*G*), holes (*H*, *I*).

Current flow ⟶

Running a Rapid.   The illustration shows a rapid that might confront an oarsman. He can choose from two downstream Vs, one of which (A) leads into some shallow rocks (C) just under the water and may hang up the boat. The boatman decides to enter in the other V (B). As soon as he is in the rapid he begins to ferry to the right. He can use the eddy behind the boulders (D) at the top of the rapid to help move the boat across. When he reaches the large waves (E), he makes his ferry angle less so as not to take on too much water. Upon reaching the narrow slot between the rock (F) and the shore, he ships both oars. Then as soon as he is past the slot, he pulls hard to the left, but is barely able to miss a group of boulders (G). So he does a back pivot, quickly pulling hard on his right oar, and runs backward. He does not have time to turn around and runs some holes (H) straight on backward. Then immediately after the holes, he turns the back end of the boat and pulls to the inside of the curve to avoid the huge holes against the cliff (I). Once past the cliff and the last obstacles, the passenger pats the oarsman on the back and the oarsman pulls off and waits for the rest of his party.

SAFETY, HAZARDS, RESCUE, AND EMERGENCY REPAIRS

It was a cold and windy day on the Salt River in Arizona. We had expected warm weather on the desert river located eighty miles east of Phoenix, Arizona, but instead it had snowed.

When Fran, who had been sitting in the raft all day, stepped out on shore at our campsite, she stumbled. I asked her if she felt all right. She drowsily replied that she just wanted to rest.

Nothing was out of the ordinary: it had been a long day in the rafts and kayaks, and we all were a little stiff. But the conditions were ripe for hypothermia, and remaining concerned, I started a fire and began to prepare hot drinks.

We convinced her to slip into a sleeping bag near the fire. As she lay in the bag, I asked her questions, and she slowly answered some, but then stopped and mumbled, "Just let me sleep." Perhaps, I thought to myself, I was carrying this hypothermia thing a little too far. All she wanted to do was sleep. But I continued chatting with her and when she remained drowsy, John, another member of our party, crawled in with her and covered both of them with more sleeping bags.

Once she looked up at me and said, "Oh, you just came into focus." It was then I finally was sure that she did, in fact, have hypothermia. Her distorted perception of reality meant that her internal body temperature was dangerously low and we had to warm her quickly to prevent her from slipping further into hypothermia's dangerous life-sapping spiral, which leads to death. We removed the last of her damp clothing, and John stripped bare and huddled with her. When Jerry put Fran's feet against his bare stomach, she finally began to recover.

Later, Fran felt better and sat with us around the fire chatting. But that night everyone was gun-shy of the cold, and we all lined up our bags in a row and snuggled together, savoring each other's warmth on the cold, frosty night.

Though the trip was cold, it was one of the most memorable river trips

I have ever had. I have a photo of our party posing in front of our kayaks with snow-covered hills in the background. On the bottom of the kayak in the foreground, outlined with strips of duct tape, we wrote, "Ski the Salt River." But the trip easily could have turned into a tragedy had we not been alert to dangers such as hypothermia. Whether a river is class I or class V, wet and cold are two of the most common hazards facing river runners.

Wetness, cold, and fatigue are primary causes of hypothermia.

Hypothermia

Hypothermia can occur in a number of different situations. It usually is associated with cold, rainy days, but also can happen on warm days when someone takes a chilly swim in cold water. On one trip on a class I river in high water, the boat I was in hit a stump and flipped over, spilling us into the cold, early spring runoff water. I grabbed a pack and paddle and started to swim to shore, which was only ten yards away. Suddenly, my arms felt very heavy and it became harder to swim. I let go of the pack and paddle and had to use all of my remaining strength to get to shore. When I reached the edge, my companions, fortunately, were there to drag me onto shore, for I was so weak by then that I could not get out of the water. I had been in the river less than five minutes, and yet on shore I could not even unbutton my clothes without help.

Many boaters underestimate what cold river water can do. When the water is cold and weather conditions are poor, wet suits are by far the best means of protection. Kayakers, of course, should in most cases wear wet suits anyway. For more information on clothing, see the "Day and Overnight Equipment" chapter.

Symptoms. Whether you have been dunked in the river, are wet from splashing waves or rain, or are just plain cold, hypothermia is the overriding concern. Hypothermia is a lowering of the body's core temperature, the end result of which is death. Hypothermia can occur as quietly and subtly as it did with Fran on the Salt River. This subtleness makes it important that you know its signs and stages:
1. Poor coordination
   Intensive shivering
   Slowing of movements
2. Continued shivering
   Stumbling
   Fatigue
   Thickness of speech
3. Decreased shivering
   Disorientation
   Memory lapses
   Hallucinations
4. Very noticeable drowsiness
   Irrationality
   Weak or irregular pulse
5. Unconsciousness
   Death

Treatment. If you recognize any of the signs of hypothermia in someone in your group, immediately move the person to the side of the river. It may be enough to get dry clothing on him, but if symptoms are more than minor, the victim probably will need external heat.

For building a fire when it is really needed in cold, wet, hypothermic weather, some type of fire starter—such as solid fuel pellets, a candle, pitch wood—always should be carried.

If suitably protected from wind, you can build a fire below the high-water mark of the river where damage to the river's environment will be minimized. If you have a stove, so much the better. Hot drinks can be readied while wet clothing is removed. *If the victim is conscious and coherent*, give him warm fluids and candy to provide quick energy.

In serious forms of hypothermia in which the victim is semiconscious or unconscious, you must act quickly. If the victim can be moved with little delay to a bath, place him in water that is 105 to 110 degrees Fahrenheit. Keep the victim's arms and legs out of the warm water. This prevents the life-threatening reaction in which cold blood from the extremities floods into the core of the body.

If no bath is available nearby or if you are in a wilderness setting, by far the best treatment, even for moderate forms of hypothermia, is to remove all the victim's clothing and get him into a sleeping bag with an unclad volunteer. Monitor the victim's breathing and pulse. Be prepared to give cardiopulmonary resuscitation (CPR). Remember, with hypothermia the victim has lost the capacity to regain normal body temperature. Putting him alone in a sleeping bag will not do the job. You need to provide him with an outside source of heat.

Prevention. It is best, of course, never to have to deal with hypothermia in the first place. Wear adequate clothing. Do not forget the chilling effect of wind, and wear wind or rain parkas. Have snacks readily available, and especially on cool trips be sure everyone is nibbling throughout the day. Keep everyone active. If you are in an oar raft, have the passengers help with rowing. Stop early; do not let the party get overly fatigued, which opens the door for hypothermia.

Unexpected Swims

If you are knocked out of an inflatable raft, kayak, or any other craft, first get to the upstream side of the boat to avoid getting caught between a rock and the boat. If the inflatable raft you have been knocked out of is still right side up, swim to it and climb back in. Inflatable rafts are not easy to crawl into, and you may need help from others in the boat.

If you are forced to swim through a rapid, keep your feet downstream in order to fend off rocks. Be cautious of rocks with slits or cracks that can entrap your feet. In forceful water it is difficult to make much of a swimming motion. Save your energy until you see an eddy that you can get to. Then, if there are no rocks, turn over on your stomach and swim hard, ferrying, for the eddy. If you are dropping through holes with lots of foam, breathing with the teeth clenched will help avoid taking in

Capsized boaters should stay on the upstream side of the craft.

mouthfuls of water.

In swift current, turn over on your stomach as you near shore and feel with your hands until you touch the bottom. Do not try to stand until you reach a point where there is no current or it is too shallow for swimming. Standing too early may cause your feet to become entrapped, as explained later in this chapter.

Capsized Rafts

Whenever a wave throws one side of the raft upward, the occupants immediately should throw their weight to the high side in an effort to keep the boat from flipping. This method may prevent many flips, but occasionally rubber boats do capsize.

On one cold and rainy river trip, we missed a scout and ran blindly through a class IV rapid with several large holes. Ahead, one of the kayakers flipped in a big hole and came out of his boat. The flotation bag deflated, and in the midst of the rapid, I had a quick glance of the kayak, standing vertically as it rounded the corner. I hit the huge hole in my raft and luckily washed through, but the raft behind me flipped. Then another flipped, and another. In all, that one rapid flipped three out of our five rafts and badly damaged the kayak.

Flips often occur because boaters do not scout the river ahead, as happened to us. Careful planning frequently can prevent capsizing. At other times, no amount of advance planning can prevent a flip—your boat is just in the wrong place at the wrong time. Flips can occur in holes or by hitting trees, tree stumps, bridge piers, or rocks. Always prepare for flips by being sure that gear is securely lashed.

Always be prepared for flips by securely lashing everything down.

Try to jump clear of any obstructions in the river if the boat goes over. Get out from underneath the boat if you find yourself there. Deaths have occurred when people have become trapped under inflatable rafts that have flipped. Check to be sure that no one else is underneath. If the rapid is severe and you find yourself close to any eddy, your best bet may be to leave the boat and go for the safety of the side of the river. If not, get to the upstream side of the boat. It may spin around and you will be forced to move from position to position to stay on the upstream side. If possible, climb on top of the overturned raft.

Using flip lines to right a raft

Flip lines are very handy items, especially on small rafts. They are long enough to stretch across the width of the bottom of the boat and are tied to D rings on the side of the boat. When not in use, the lines are held in a small coil with a strip of inner tube or a quick-release knot. If the boat flips, the lines can be tossed over to the other side of the flipped raft and a person on the opposite side can use it to help him climb on top. He then can help the other swimming rafters onto the overturned boat. Once the boat reaches safe, deep water, the rafters can grab the flip lines, place their feet on the opposite tube, and throw the weight of their bodies backward. As the rafters fall into the water, the raft will flip right side up. It always is important to be sure the boat is not passing over any shallow rocks as this is done.

I watched Tolly Tollefson flip her small Avon in a huge hole in the Colorado River's House Rocks Rapids, but at the end of the rapids, she crawled on the capsized boat and with flip lines, single-handledly righted her raft. Then she grabbed the oars, picked up her passenger, and continued down the river.

If the boat is not uprighted by flip lines, you will want to get it to the side of the river. In a capsized paddle boat, the paddlers may jump on and use their paddles, which they should hang onto in a flip, and paddle to shore. Or one person can swim ashore with the bow or stern line (normally three-eighths-inch polypropylene). If the bow and stern lines are each contained in a throw bag, the process is easier. Some boaters who are running rivers where capsizing is likely, attach a separate, special throw bag with a three-hundred-foot, quarter-inch polypropylene emergency beaching line to the side of the boat.

In many cases another boat in the party can nudge and push the capsized craft to shore.

Kayak Self-Rescue

The kayaker's best form of self-rescue is the roll. Even in easy white water, being able to roll increases your confidence and your ability to prevent unwanted swims. Always try several attempts at the roll before bailing out. The boat sometimes will be positioned wrongly in the current, and subsequent roll attempts will swing it around to a position where the current will help the roll.

Even the best kayakers sometimes have to swim. When the swim occurs, you may do one or more of the following:

- If you find yourself in a dangerous, turbulent rapid and if an eddy can be reached, abandon the boat and go for it.
- If you are not close to any eddies, it may be best to hold onto the boat to help provide more flotation. Always keep the boat downstream of you to fend off rocks. Do not let your feet get caught by rocks under the river. Hold onto the paddle if you can. Ride out the rapid until you get to a spot where you can swim to shore.
- Most sources suggest that you leave the kayak upside down since it will trap air inside and keep the boat from filling with water. But air bags will provide more than enough flotation, and the kayak will be bucked and turned and probably will fill with water anyway. When you get close to an eddy or reach a calm section, hold the grab loop and kick and sidestroke to

A capsized kayaker swimming his boat to shore. To make the process easier, the paddle can be shoved in the cockpit. The kayaker, now having full use of his arms, pushes the boat toward shore, swims to it, and continues pushing and swimming until reaching the shore.

shore. If holding onto the boat will cause you to drop into another rapid, forget the boat and get yourself out.

- A good method to use when you are out of rough water is to turn the kayak right side up and jam your paddle inside the cockpit. Push the kayak toward the side, swim to it and push it again, alternating swimming and pushing until you are to the shore. In this way you have total use of your arms to make swimming more efficient, and your kayak and paddle are together in case they get away from you. If conditions permit, some boaters, no matter what the difficulty of the water, will jam their paddle inside the cockpit, assuring them that the kayak and paddle always will be together.

Assisted Kayak Rescue

In difficult rapids it is not easy for a kayaker still in his boat to help a swimmer. Often you have to wait until the rapid eases before the swimmer can grab a hold of your kayak and you can pull him to safety. Charlie Walbridge, a well-known white-water enthusiast in the eastern United States and an authority on white-water safety, frequently has pointed out that in a difficult rapid one or more boaters holding throw bags (see the "Rope Rescue" section later in this chapter) on the side of the river are probably the best form of rescue. It also is a good idea to use this method with beginning boaters who are apt to swim in less difficult rapids.

Always leave the boat for others and rescue the paddler first, having him hold the grab loop while you paddle hard toward an eddy on the side. The swimmer can help greatly by kicking his feet.

There are several ways to get a kayak off to the side. You can nudge the abandoned kayak with the bow of your boat, trying to push it to the side of the river. If the boat is right side up, you can put your nose into the cockpit hole, and paddle until the boat is off to the side.

Nudging the boat often is difficult and in fast water it may be miles before the rescuer can get the abandoned boat off to the side. Several other methods are used by kayakers. One is to use an eight-foot length of quarter- to three-eighths-inch polypropylene rope with a carabiner tied to

A capsized kayaker can hold the grab loops and be pulled ashore.

A boat can be nudged to the side of the river, though this is difficult in fast-moving water.

one end and the other end tied to a loop of two-inch-wide flat webbing (available from mountaineering shops). The loop of webbing is slipped around one shoulder and the carabiner is clipped in the grab loop of the kayak. If any trouble develops and you must get rid of the abandoned kayak, just let go of the paddle and let the loop slip off your shoulder and arm.

Bruce Mason of the University of Oregon outdoor program uses a belt made of two-inch-wide flat webbing. The belt is held around the waist over the spray skirt by means of Velcro so it can be released easily if for some reason the rescuer must leave the abandoned boat.

Both methods are much easier than nudging the boat, but in any method a rescuer always should be sure that he easily can release the abandoned boat and that there is no way that he can become entangled in the rope used for the rescue.

Getting Paddles to the Side. There is little problem getting paddles to the side if the swimming kayaker has jammed his paddle inside the cockpit. If a swimming boater is relatively safe, he should hold onto his paddle.

If you must pick up an abandoned paddle, there are a couple of methods you can use to try to get it to shore.

- Put the two paddles together and paddle to shore as if they were one paddle.
- Put the blade of the paddle against the front of the cockpit rim and lay the shaft on your shoulder. Hold it in place with your chin and in that contorted position, paddle to the side.
- In easy water, release the spray skirt and place the paddle partly inside the front of your boat so that it passes by your side and sticks out behind you. Be sure the paddle does not trap your feet in the kayak. This method gives you room to paddle relatively freely.

Rope Rescue

A rescue sling is used to pull an overturned boat ashore.

Ropes are the most important tool for river rescue and should be carried in every boat. They can be used to haul in passengers who have been washed out of an inflatable raft, to land boats, to pull equipment across the river, to help an exhausted boater across the river, to assist a boater stranded on a mid-river rock, to hold a victim's head above water when his feet are entrapped, to rescue a boater caught in a hole, to pull a swimmer to safety during a bad swim, as well as for many other uses.

The primary guideline when using ropes is: *Never tie yourself or anyone else to a rope.* Deaths have occurred when people have attempted to haul another person tied to a rope across a river. Even with a life jacket on, a person tied to a rope planes underwater like a diving paper airplane and remains underwater. Whether you are on shore or in the water, hold onto the rope or a loop tied on the rope, but never wrap the rope around your hand or put your wrist through the loop. A sudden tightening of the rope can entangle you and pull you under. By holding onto the rope, you simply can let go if any problems develop.

Throwing a Rope.   For most conditions, by far the simplest of throwing ropes are those enclosed in a nylon bag called a *throw bag*, a marvelous, simple tool that prevents rope entanglements, saves rescuers precious time, and can be used by relatively unskilled individuals. To throw a throw bag, pull out the top of the rope from the bag and hold it with the nonthrowing hand. As an extra precaution, you also can step on the end. Grasp the bag and throw it underhanded. The rope will play out easily. If you must throw the bag again, pull in the rope, letting it pile up alongside you. Leave some water in the bag for some weight, and throw it again.

In extremely cold conditions the rope in a throw bag can freeze, preventing the bag from functioning properly. On such cold trips, a rope should be carried. Even if you are boating during warmer times, it still is wise to know how to handle a rope. A rope not in a throw bag can be prepared for throwing in two ways. Some coil the rope in the same way as a climbing rope is coiled. Start with the end that is thrown to the victim. Give the rope a slight twist as you coil it to make the loops neat and orderly without knots. With polypropylene line, the best rope for river rescue, it is difficult to keep the coils from twisting, but fortunately, the rope is stiff enough to be usable.

Another way of preparing the rope for throwing is to start with the end that you are throwing to the victim. Place that end in your throwing hand,

The throw bag is by far the best method of storing and throwing a rope. The boater pictured is holding the bag by the drawstring, but to throw it he will grasp the bag by the edge of the opening and throw it with an underhanded motion.

A.   B.

A fast, effective way of coiling rope for throwing is to lay bights or loops of rope alternately on each side of the hand, making a butterfly coil.

In throwing a rope that has been coiled, one-half to two-thirds of the coils are placed in the nonthrowing hand. The remaining coils are thrown with a straight arm, underhand motion. Standing on the end of the rope that is not thrown is a wise precaution.

When throwing a rope, lead the throw ahead of the downstream-moving target in order to get the rope to the capsized boater.

then make a loop or bight approximately two feet long. Hold the loop with the throwing hand. Then make another loop the same size but on the opposite side of the hand. Continue making bights. The advantage of making bights is that the rope can be prepared much quicker, and during the throw, the rope plays out easily.

To throw a rope prepared by either of these methods, place one-half to two-thirds of the coils or bights in the nonthrowing hand. Throw the remaining coils or bights with the throwing hand using a straight-arm, underhand motion. O. K. Goodwin, the safety chairman of the American Whitewater Affiliation (Big Bar, California), emphasizes that the straight arm and the underhand motion are vital for a good throw. Allow the coils from the nonthrowing hand to play out as the rope sails through the air.

As an extra precaution, before throwing, step on the end of the rope that stays with you in case you accidentally let go with the nonthrowing hand. Throwing a rope is a skill that is developed with practice, and it will not be effective unless you spend considerable time at home coiling and tossing a rope. Fifty feet is an average range for most throwers.

Precautions. Keep your life jacket on whenever throwing a rope. If you have gloves, use them. Before tossing the rope, yell "rope" to be sure the swimmer is aware that you are throwing it. Charlie Walbridge writes that "most people who are in trouble in rapids are disoriented and can't see the rope or hear a yell over the roar of the rapid. The only sure way to get their attention is to try to hit them in the face." Hitting the victim involves a bit of timing. The current is sweeping him downstream and while the bag is in the air after the toss, he can be swept past where the bag is going to land. In other words, you have to *lead your throw* so that you hit the downstream-moving target. If you make an error in the throw, it is better to err by leading slightly too much since a rope downstream of a swimmer is easier to reach than one behind.

Thrower's position. On segments of a rapid where trouble may occur, position yourself with a throw rope below the problem area. Find a secure location where you will not be toppled over. Keep in mind that when a swimmer grabs the rope he will swing in a wide arc to a point farther downstream from where you stand. Try to make that point an eddy and not a ledge or a downed tree. If additional help is available, they should move down to that point to assist the victim.

Belay. A belay is a means of holding a rope while a swimmer grasps the other end. In a belay, the rope is passed around the back of the waist. The hand on the side on which the rope is piled during the belay is the breaking hand. The other hand helps guide the rope. The breaking hand is never taken off the rope. By gripping with this hand the rope is stopped, and by loosening the grip, the rope slides through. O. K. Goodwin recommends belaying from a sitting position since the pull usually is greater than expected.

Any slack existing in the rope after throwing can be pulled in quickly by using both hands. When the rope is taut, go back into the belay position. In this position, be sure the rope does not get tangled around any parts of the body. Be ready to get rid of it if you are pulled out of your stance.

Boulders and trees also can be used as more powerful—and safer—belays. Pass the rope around a rounded edge of a boulder or the side of a tree, using caution not to become entangled in rope.

Victim. The victim should swim to the rope and immediately grab it. The rope should be held tightly, but it should never be wrapped around

In a body belay, do not let the rope get tangled around legs or arms and be ready to get rid of the rope if necessary.

Using a boulder or tree is safer than a body belay.

a hand or arm. Some people recommend turning away from the thrower as soon as it is grasped and draping the rope over the shoulder, bracing for the shock that comes when the rope goes taut. At any rate, expect to be pulled under as the rope tightens. If you are holding onto a kayak or inflatable raft, put both the rope and the boat in the same hand, rather than in opposite hands, which will feel like you are being pulled apart.

Other Points. If the rope is used to pull someone out of a hole, especially a long hole that extends across the river (such as the hydraulic below a dam), pull the person sideways across the length of the hole. It may be impossible from a position downstream to pull the person through the strong backwash.

If you are trying to reach a stranded person on a rock in the river, Walbridge suggests ferrying out to him in a raft. Or in the case of a kayak party, ferry to the rock and have the stranded person crawl on the rear deck of a kayak, wrapping his arms and legs around the boat to stay on. This type of rescue is expedited by a Blackadar handle—a small handle that a stranded boater can hold onto just behind the cockpit.

In the last resort if the person is very exhausted, Walbridge suggests

If washed broadside into a rock or cliff, lean into it. This kayaker has erred by leaning upstream. If there is any danger of entrapment, he should eject himself from the kayak immediately.

that a rescuer should be sent out to him. The rescuer holds the throw rope in one hand and with the other arm holds the exhausted victim in a cross chest carry as he brings him across.

Broaching

Kayak Broaching. If your kayak is being washed up against a rock, always make a last effort stroke. It may be enough to push the boat off along the side of the cushion. If it does not work, immediately lean toward (against) the rock. You want to keep the onrushing water from catching your deck and flipping you upstream. As you lean you may be able to push with the paddle or one hand to get off the rock. If the kayak tips upstream or starts folding, get out quickly before it collapses and entraps you.

Inflatable Raft Broaching. As in kayaking, try to make a last effort to pull around the side. If you start a spin just before you hit the rock, the momentum may help the raft bounce off the rock. You also may be able to hit the rock directly with your bow. If there are passengers or paddlers in the stern when the bow hits, they quickly should move forward toward the bow so that the onrushing current does not push the stern under. Anytime a raft is washed sideways into a rock, all paddlers or passengers immediately should lean into the rock to take their weight off the upstream tube. If none of these methods works and you are stuck broadside against the rock, quickly jump to the side of the boat against the rock. This move will help prevent the upstream tube from plunging under the water, seriously pinning the boat.

When broached, you may be able to push against the rock, pry with oars or paddles, bounce and jerk the boat, or pull with the one free oar or paddle to get the boat off. If that does not work, move people to the side of the boat that is farthest out in the current. Failing that, it is possible to make a drogue or sea anchor by tying boat bags together. The boat bags thrown into the current have tremendous pull and may be able to pull the boat off. The pull is so great that you should double up the rope and securely lash gear, or it may be lost. If all these methods fail, or your boat is hopelessly wrapped around the rock, you will need rope assistance from shore.

Pinned Boats

If a kayak, inflatable raft, or other craft is wrapped and pinned on a rock, evaluate the situation. One side of the craft usually will be exposed to more current than the other side. Try to rig your ropes to take advantage of this. Tie ropes to the side that is affected by less current, trying to pull this side upstream, preferably from the opposite shore. In this way, the longer side is pried in the direction that the current is naturally pushing it. A second rope should be attached to help pull the boat into shore when it comes loose.

Ropes can be attached to grab loops on kayaks or may even be tied all around the kayak. On inflatable rafts, tie them to D rings, or, if you have to, cut a slit in the floor and tie the ropes around the tube. Try to tie ropes so that as pull is exerted from upstream, the boat rolls sideways, exposing less surface area to the current.

Removing a raft pinned to a rock

For pulling pinned boats off rocks, it is best to avoid nylon ropes. Nylon stretches and if it breaks or a D ring tears off, the rope springs back dangerously. The ideal rope for river rescue—rope that is strong, stretches little, and floats—does not exist. The best is a compromise. Manila, a natural fiber, stretches little but varies in strength according to the type of manila. It also rots in time, especially with river use, and does not float. Polyester ropes have the least stretch of the synthetics, but they also do not float. That leaves polypropylene. Certain weaves, such as a braid-on-braid weave, of polypropylene rope have less stretch and more strength than other weaves. A good choice for river rescue is Dualine, a floating, low-stretch rope marketed by Voyageur's (see the "Equipment" section of the "Sources" chapter), with a braid-on-braid weave that incorporates a nylon jacket for strength and abrasion resistance along with a polypropylene interior.

No matter what type of rope is used, the forces generated by moving water are tremendous and a sudden jerk by a boat becoming free, or a surge by the current, can pull rescuers out of their stances. *Do not allow any of the rope to wrap around any parts of your body.* Warn others. In at least two cases I have heard about, boatmen who were pulling pinned boats off rocks lost fingers that had been caught in the rope. Use extreme caution.

To exert the force necessary to pull the boat off, a number of people can grasp the rope and pull, or you can use a winch. On stubbornly pinned boats, you may have to deflate one side. If that does not work, part of the floor can be cut out to lessen the water resistance.

Getting rafts off rocks can be extremely difficult, especially those in midstream in deep, swiftly moving water. You may be limited to only one side of the river from which you can pull. Differing situations require ingenuity and imagination. But remember, it is only gear; do not risk anyone's life trying to get it off.

Entrapment

Entrapment can be broken into three basic types, which we will examine more closely.

Trapped in a Boat. In most cases, this applies to kayakers since their legs can be trapped under the deck if it collapses for some reason. But rafters in a boat that folds around a rock should get clear of it at all costs.

The most common situation occurs when a kayak is washed up against a rock or trees and the onrushing current collapses the deck, trapping the boater inside. Another situation is when a kayak plunges over a small drop and its bow gets caught between boulders on the bottom of the river. If the boat is held fast, the deck may collapse around the paddler's legs.

The best prevention is for a kayaker always to use full-length foam walls or pillars to prevent the deck from collapsing. Normally he should attempt to stay in the boat since this is safest, but if the boat becomes pinned and the current is dangerously fast, Walbridge advises that he eject immediately.

In rescuing someone pinned in a boat, you may find it difficult to get to him. If you can, it may be possible to break and rip open the boat to free him. A skin diver's knife with a sawlike blade may be useful in attempting to cut him out.

Swimmer Trapped in Downed Trees or Snags. Downed trees or strainers, as we noted in the "Reading White Water" chapter, are dangerous because they allow water, but not boats, to flow through. Watch also for undercut rocks, bridge piers that are close together, brush, and split rocks.

The best precaution is to stay in the boat, for as long as you are there, you can maneuver around strainers. Watch the outside of river bends, give log jams a safe berth, and be particularly careful in small streams. Scout blind corners.

If you suddenly round a corner or come up from a roll and find yourself just about to be swept into a tree, some boaters suggest jumping out of the boat and attempting to get through the strainers without the handicap of your boat. Walt Blackadar was an advocate of this method. On a small stream we ran, he jumped out of his boat and was able to grab a bush hanging in the river to save himself from being swept into a downed tree blocking the entire river channel.

If you are swimming and are washed into a snag, hit it head on and try to work through. Do not hold onto any branches. Keep your momentum going. On some trees you may grab for a higher branch and pull yourself up over the top of it.

Rescue is extremely difficult. In some cases, the branches of the tree literally can tie knots around a person. On one trip I was on, a two-man-kayak team was washed into the bushes on the outside of the bank of a class I river. The paddlers escaped, but it took several hours of work with ropes and saws to get the boat loose from the tangle of branches.

Try to get to the person if the water is not too deep. Do not endanger yourself. Get a rope out to him by approaching from the downstream side of the strainer. Because it may be the only way to keep the victim's head above water, this is one of the rare situations where you would tie a rope on the victim. Tie it underneath the arms and have someone from shore keep his head above water. When the victim is breathing, then attempt to untangle him.

Foot of Victim Lodged between Rocks in Bottom of River. When a foot of a boater standing in swift water becomes accidentally lodged between two boulders, the current may topple him over and hold him under the water. Unfortunately, a number of deaths have occurred due to this type of entrapment. Even a life jacket will not keep the head above water if the current is swift.

The best precaution is not to try to stand in swiftly moving water. Swim until you get near shore, then reach down with your hands and be sure the water is very shallow before standing. Always use caution when attempting to free pinned boats or to land boats, or in other situations where you may have to stand in moving water.

Rescue, as with entrapment in downed trees, is very difficult. If you can get to the victim in this situation, you also tie him to a rope and have those on shore attempt to keep his head above water. When you are sure the victim is breathing, then work on getting his foot free.

Boat Caught in a Hole

Oar Boat.   When an oar boat is caught in a hole, the passengers and oarsman should move to the downstream side of the boat. If it is possible to row, try to pull the boat out of the hole to one side. Or try holding the oar deep in the water to catch the downstream flow of current to help push you out. If these attempts fail, get a rope from shore and see if your mates can pull you out. One last move is to cut the floor of the raft.

Paddle Boat.   If a paddle boat is caught in a hole, all paddlers should move to the downstream side and brace with their paddles. Try to reach over the curling-back foam and catch downstream water to pull the boat out, or attempt to paddle the boat to the side of the hole. If these attempts do not work, try to get a rescue rope from shore to pull the boat out.

Kayak.   When caught, keep leaning and bracing downstream. Attempt to reach over the curling-back foam and catch the downstream current. Often it is not possible, so try to work to the side. If this does not work, deliberately capsize the kayak and hang down in the boat, attempting to catch onto the downstream current to flush you out. Try to hang on upside down for a while. Most kayakers do not hang down long enough for them to be washed out. When you feel the washing machine feeling subside, you probably will be out; then roll. The last resort is to eject yourself and dive deeply so the current can carry you free.

Swimmer Caught in a Hole

Swimmer Self-Rescue.   If you are out of your boat and caught in a hole, try to conserve as much strength as possible by not making any unnecessary, flailing motions. If your boat is caught with you in the hole, hang onto it for it may pull you out. I once watched a friend of mine caught in a hole. We had time to get out of our kayaks and start working our way back up to him with a rope. His boat finally started out, and he grabbed it and was pulled to safety.

While in the hole, breathe through your teeth to help filter air through the foamy water. To get out of a hole, assume a spread-eagle position. Allow the current to bring you back upstream. As you get to the crest of the reversal and when you feel the current force you down, dive for the bottom in an attempt to reach the downstream current underneath the

Kayaker caught in a hole. He eventually tipped upside down and was washed out.

surface turbulence. It is because of this situation that some boaters prefer less buoyant life jackets. However, most knowledgeable boaters claim that the power of the current in a hole far outweighs the buoyancy of a life jacket, so it makes little difference. Some boaters have advocated taking the life jacket off to enable you to dive deeply in the river. But most boaters caution against such a radical move. If you get out of the hole without a life jacket, it is likely that you will have to swim through more rapids in an extremely exhausted state and may never make it to the surface. In the great majority of natural situations, a hole will not hold a person for long. Dams, however, are a different story.

Dams. The hydraulic created below a dam is extremely dangerous. If you are caught in it, use the method described for getting out of natural holes: allow the current to circulate you back to the edge of the dam and when the water pushes you down, dive for the bottom. If you hit the bottom, Walbridge advises that you spring back up with the feet angling downstream.

For rescues of victims caught in holes, and especially in the hydraulics formed below dams, stay in the darker, downstream-moving current. Some rescuers who have ventured too close to the white, hydraulic current have been drawn and fatally trapped with the victims.

Rescue by Other Boaters. It may be difficult to get to a person caught in a hole. You may be able to row a boat up behind the hole or the dam. But, Walbridge warns, you must at all costs stay in the darker, downstream-moving current. If the boat is allowed to touch the white foaming water behind the hole, your boat may be sucked upstream, entrapping you also. There actually have been a number of deaths of rescuers that have occurred under these same circumstances. Try to get a throw rope to the person trapped. Tying a life jacket to it will help make it more visible so he may grab it.

River First Aid

Besides being aware of hypothermia, a boater needs to be prepared for a variety of first aid problems that can occur on rivers. It is important to know how to do mouth-to-mouth artificial respiration; to care for open wounds, shock, and snake bites; and to perform other first aid. The best procedure is to take an advanced first aid course. Since shoulder dislocations are a common injury among kayakers, consult a doctor before undertaking wilderness trips and learn how to reduce a dislocation.

On wilderness trips where you are gone for several days or weeks, you need to be particularly well prepared. See "Checklists" at the end of the book for a listing of items in a first aid kit. One excellent medical source is James Wilkerson's *Medicine for Mountaineering* (see the "Books" section of the "Sources" chapter).

Getting Help

If a serious accident occurs, you and your group will need to put your heads together and formulate a plan of action. There is no set procedure; you need to consider the weather, the river, the number of people in your party, and other factors in order to make a decision. Here are some possibilities:

- In many cases, an injured person may be floated off the river and then transported to a place where he can receive medical care.
- If the injury is more serious, you may have to summon help. The river offers a quick passageway and a boat that constantly is paddled or oared downriver can get off most rivers in a day. Once off the river, a helicopter or other help may be called.
- You may be able to flag down another boat and ask for assistance. On most rivers you will find other boaters or doctors on float trips who can help.
- With three signal fires, three flares, a signal mirror, and/or the forming of a large, colorful X on the ground with life jackets, clothing, or gear, you can attempt to attract a passing aircraft. Do not underestimate the value of a signal mirror; they do work, as many people can attest.

Whatever the situation, do not start running the river expecting a rescue to be readily available. Be adequately prepared. If outside help is summoned, be prepared to pay all the rescue expenses.

Raft Damage

It is not too difficult to repair rafts at home, but often you must repair them while on a river. To complicate matters, it can be raining. If it is and there is no way of limping into camp, pull the boat off and set up tarps or rain flies to provide shelter both for the boat and the party. Most glues for patching work much better in warm conditions, so it is helpful to have a fire or stove going. But build the fire away from the work area and be extremely careful: glues and solvents are flammable. One way of warming glue is to boil water in a pot and put the glue container in the warm water. Some people heat a Dutch oven lid to provide a source of heat.

Different types of glues are compatible with different types of materials. Also, some raft materials require a special patching procedure,

Be prepared by having the knowledge and carrying first aid supplies to handle problems on the river.

so it is always a good idea to find out from the manufacturer how to repair the boat before you buy it. The basic procedure involves cutting a patch one-half to one inch larger than the length and width of the rip. Thoroughly rough up both the patch and the ripped area of the raft by rubbing them with sandpaper or by scraping a knife across the material. The next step is important and left out by many. Take solvent that is recommended by the manufacturer (carbon tetrachloride, if no other information is available) and clean both the roughed up surfaces. Coat the glue on the patch and raft, following the directions on the glue container. Wait for the glue to set before applying the patch. Do not rush this part—it is essential to a good patching job.

Also be prepared to fix split oars, cracked frames, broken oarlocks, and so on. Often duct tape or bailing wire can make temporary repairs. When you are preparing for the trip at home, be sure to include various repair tools and materials in a kit (see the "Day and Overnight Equipment" chapter and "Checklists" at the end of the book). Without them a boater may find himself helpless.

Kayak Damage

Again, with damaged kayaks different types of materials may demand different types of repair procedures. A good manufacturer supplies the necessary repair information with his boats. Often, kayak damage can be temporarily repaired with duct tape. I have paddled with friends who essentially had destroyed their kayaks, but with enough duct tape, they managed to run the rest of the river with their craft. A handy hint for repairing kayaks in wet weather, suggested by Walbridge, is to apply wet suit glue to the patch area, light it on fire, and apply duct tape. The tape will not come loose.

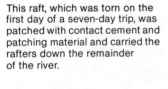

This raft, which was torn on the first day of a seven-day trip, was patched with contact cement and patching material and carried the rafters down the remainder of the river.

PLANNING MULTI-DAY TRIPS

The portal of the gorge lay ahead of us. Floating on quiet water, we could not mistake the great gash in the towering walls where the river disappeared. It was the entrance of the canyon that we had had on our minds since the beginning of the trip. We had no idea of what type of white water we might encounter on this portion of the river, located in a remote part of the Yukon Territory in Canada. No one before us had ever run it.

My boating companion, Jerry Dixon, and I pulled our kayaks up on shore at the entrance to the canyon. We worked our way on and around cliffs and across talus fields, scouting the rapids in the river below. The first part looked good: some class IV water, but nothing that we could not handle in the maneuverable, inflatable kayaks, specially designed with a covered deck and a fiber glass cockpit to keep out splashing water. We hiked on, finding more runnable rapids but no suitable place to stop between rapids. The canyon walls plunged straight into the river and in some places overhung the water. We scoured the sides of the river looking for a break in the walls, but we could not find a single weakness where a kayak could be beached and we could get out.

Then the gorge narrowed dramatically into a twisting slot not much wider than a doorway. A huge pile of torn and splintered logs and driftwood had lodged against the canyon walls, forming an imposing, spiny plug rising fifty feet above the water. The river was so narrow here that Jerry rappelled to the edge and straddled the canyon with feet on opposite canyon walls.

Even though the river was runnable to this point, we could find no place where we could get out of our boats to carry them around the huge driftwood plug blocking our run through the gorge. We were left no choice but to portage the entire two-and-a-half-mile stretch of the canyon. Fortunately, the equipment that we had chosen was suitable for the river. From our aerial reconnaissance we had known that long portages might be required. The inflatable kayaks could be deflated and, along with their fiber glass seats, stuffed into a pack for the long, difficult portage across steep, loose-scree slopes, dense and tangled brush, and exposed, precipitous cliffs. Even with our lightweight equipment, the portage took two and a half days to complete. With fiber glass kayaks or inflatable rafts, the portage would have been many times more arduous.

Choice of equipment, then, becomes an important consideration when planning multi-day river trips. The following section looks more closely at this aspect of planning.

Styles of Craft

Going light—for some, a way of simplifying the river experience

Whether you plan a trip on a remote river in the Yukon Territory or a river close to home, you will want to choose the craft you float and the type of equipment you carry to match the river. For the purposes of this book, let's consider two basic "styles" of running rivers—lightweight and luxurious—falling on opposite ends of a spectrum. The type of river you plan to run and how much comfort you wish to have will determine the style.

Lightweight Style. The type of craft used in this style includes light, small inflatable rafts, kayaks, canoes, and other small inflatable boats such as inflatable kayaks.

Accessory camping equipment carried along includes lightweight sleeping bags, nylon tents or tarps, and other equipment that a backpacker commonly would use. Food consists of freeze-dried suppers, and lightweight lunches and breakfasts. Cooking is done on small backpacking gas stoves, or if it is environmentally acceptable, over a campfire with light cooking gear. Equipment is carried in waterproof vinyl or rubber bags or packs.

Types of trips in this category include self-contained kayak trips where everything for the trip, including food and gear, is carried in the kayak. A self-contained trip in a hard-hulled white-water kayak is the ultimate means of running white-water rivers. Boaters using this method have run extremes in white-water difficulty in remote areas. One of the most famous river journeys in a self-contained kayak was done by the late Walt Blackadar, a physician from Idaho. He challenged the enormous, turbulent, unrelenting rapids of Turnback Canyon on the Alsek River in northern British Columbia. He tried to interest other good kayakers in accompanying him, but all readily turned down his offer when they learned of the expected 50,000-cfs flow of violent water crashing between canyon walls on a river never run before. Blackadar, carrying all his gear, including his familiar plastic bottle of vodka, successfully ran the river alone.

Blackadar's trip is on the far end of the spectrum of white-water journeys and most boaters find great enjoyment running rivers far less difficult than Turnback Canyon. Blackadar's use of the self-contained kayak, however, is an excellent method of doing river trips. Equipment is light and honed to the bare minimum, and a group of kayakers working together efficiently can cover a lot of ground in a day.

Other types of trips that fit in this category include lightweight wilderness canoe trips, especially those journeys that include long portages over trailless terrain. Boaters using small (approximately less than twelve feet in size) inflatable rafts and other small inflatables can incorporate this style to run rivers. The inflatable kayaks we used in the Yukon Territory were perfectly suited for the type of river we ran.

The lightweight style is used for exploring rivers in remote territories as well as for running small, rocky rivers where lightness and maneuverability are paramount. Some boaters use this style for any river, small or large, because to them it is a way of trimming down to the raw essentials and challenging nature in a simple, meaningful way.

Luxurious Style. This style includes all forms of white-water craft, including the largest of inflatable rafts. All of the smaller craft—kayaks, canoes, and inflatables—require a sizable raft for support to carry all the equipment.

Equipment carried on luxury trips can consist of just about anything someone might take with them on a car-camping trip, minus the trailer. Large, heavy tents, sleeping bags, clothing, and even cots for people who do not like to sleep on the ground may be carried. Big stoves with large propane tanks may be used. If cooking is done over fires, large, metal fire pans are utilized to contain the ashes. Meals on such trips can be anything prepared at home, or even what you might find in the finest of restaurants. Fresh vegetables, fruits, and meats are carried in coolers packed with ice. Cooking is done in the heaviest of cookware: cast-iron ovens and pans. Heavy boxes of metal or wood are used for storage of gear and food. Some people on luxurious trips take electric pumps for bailing out water in boats, lawn chairs in which to relax by the river, and volleyball nets for recreation.

For this style of trip, the river must be large enough in volume to float larger inflatable rafts—thus, it is a popular style on larger rivers that usually do not have portages. If there are portages, the task of carrying boats and equipment is not pleasant. This style is particularly enjoyable for kayaking. All the food and overnight gear is carried on the rafts, leaving the kayaks light and maneuverable for pleasurable river running.

Some wilderness purists shun the invasion of modern conveniences and petty comforts on wild rivers. Others, however, incorporate both worlds in their repertoire of river experiences: on one trip, struggling down a remote, little-heard-of river with a minimum of equipment, yet on the next trip, kicking back in a comfortable inflatable raft, tossing Frisbees back and forth with a neighboring boat while holding onto drinks chilled with ice.

The equipment that you will have to organize and take on your overnight trip will depend on the style you choose. Obviously the lightweight style is the easiest to organize. Luxurious trips with fresh food and mountains of equipment can turn into a planning nightmare. Many trips fall someplace in between the lightweight and luxurious extremes.

Planning—First Steps

Some trips do not require much advance planning. If you know the river, it is merely a matter of throwing the equipment together and driving off to the river for the day. Other trips, however, require planning, beginning a week, maybe even months, in advance.

Because the multi-day trip demands more preparation than others, let's take a closer look at it.

Regulated Rivers. Some rivers have become so popular that the great numbers of people using them are causing problems. On popular day stretches, boats may crash into each other in rapids and kayaks may wait in lines to play at certain rapids. The most serious problems occur on rivers where overnight and multi-day trips take place. On such rivers there are only a limited number of campsites, which get used time and time again. Vegetation is trampled, campfire scars abound,

The final leg of what can be a long, anxious process: obtaining the permit to run a popular river

and human waste can cause sanitation problems. In fact, researchers on the Colorado River found that before human waste regulations were instituted, a person with a small wound on his foot could become infected with gangrene by walking across a heavily used camping beach.

To minimize environmental impact, some land agencies have been forced to develop regulations to help protect the river. The most important regulation that will affect your group on such rivers is whether or not there is a permit system.

On rivers with permit systems, you will have to apply in advance to obtain a permit. Some of these rivers have a lottery system by which names are drawn out of a hat to determine who runs the river. The important thing is to find out the various procedures involved in obtaining a permit. You will want to write far in advance; ten months is not too early.

Information about which rivers have permit systems is available in guidebooks and other sources (see the "Information Sources" section of the "Getting Started" chapter).

Assembling the Party. The group accompanying you may range from one other friend to a dozen or more people. Try to arrange trips with smaller groups—no more than a dozen. You will have fewer planning hassles, the trip will run more smoothly, and in many cases, a smaller group will cause less damage to the river's environment. In addition to your own considerations, some rivers that are managed by a governmental agency may require you to keep the party under a certain size.

If you are initiating a trip in which each of the party members runs his own boat—a kayak, canoe, or small inflatable—then everyone in the party should be sufficiently experienced for the difficulty of the river you plan to run.

On inflatable raft trips where the rafts are run by one person on the oars, inexperienced people can ride as passengers. On easy stretches of the rivers, the passengers can take turns on the oars and gradually learn how to run the boat. In this way you can put together a party with both experienced and inexperienced people.

Dispersing Information. Get your party together far in advance of the trip. Talk over dates, equipment, costs, and so on. Delegate duties. For instance, if you are short on boats, put someone in charge of renting or borrowing additional boats. If some of the party members are from out of town, send them a letter detailing the plans.

Preparation Day. A procedure followed by some float parties is to tack on at least an extra day at the beginning of the trip—before driving to the river—to spend in town, buying food, packing vehicles, and so on. The nature of a noncommercial trip is to involve everyone on the trip, and all people should help with the preparatory duties as well as river duties. This process adds a day that people may have to include in their vacation, but it makes them an integral part of the trip from start to finish. Additionally, with everyone's help, the packing, the loading, the buying of food, and the cleaning up all go much faster.

Length of Trip. Find out how long it normally takes others to run the river and adapt this amount of time to your plans. Give yourself plenty of leeway. The actual length of time that you will need on the river depends on many factors, such as how high the water is, how many (if any) portages must be made, and how many problems the party has on the journey.

Inflatable rafts in normal water conditions commonly run fifteen to twenty miles a day. A small, self-contained kayak party may average twenty-five or more miles a day.

I generally like to schedule less than the above average. That way the trip is conducted at a more relaxing pace, people become more acquainted with the river, and there is more time to hike. Putting together a multi-day trip requires a tremendous amount of energy, and once you actually get on the river, it is nice to slow down and savor the experience.

On a typical raft trip, I may average ten miles a day. On a kayak trip friends and I do on the Salmon River in Idaho, we average only three to four miles a day for the first half of the journey. This part of the Salmon is scenic and has many good rapids, ideal places in which we can play in kayaks for hours. The weather usually is warm and days are easygoing and lazy—just the way a vacation should be.

Trip Costs

Trip expenses may be fairly simple, as when you and your friends drive off and run a day's stretch on a river. Or expenses may be complicated, as when twelve-member groups embark on a two-week trip.

For efficiency, groups usually pool their money. Before leaving on a trip, make a cost estimate considering the following:

- How many vehicles will be used? What is the distance from home to the river and back? What is the distance involved in the shuttle? From the total trip mileage, estimate your gas costs.
- If you use the services of a commercial shuttle driver, add his expense.
- Based on the number of people in your group, estimate the cost of food for the entire trip.
- Add any expenses you may have in renting equipment, such as rubber boats, coolers, life jackets, tents.
- Figure expenses for group supplies. Duct tape is a common group expense since almost everyone uses it. Group repair supplies may be purchased, as well as such things as cooking pots or fire pans. If you have to fly into the river, add that expense. Some groups will pay individuals if damage occurs to rafts carrying group equipment.

Figure up the cost conservatively and then add some more to your total figure. Always collect more than you possibly will need. At the end of the trip it is an easy task to refund money, but if you end up spending more than you collect, it sometimes can be an unpleasant task to collect from everyone after the trip is finished.

If you are initiating the trip, you do not necessarily have to be the person collecting the money. Have someone else do that to spread out responsibilities. I usually stay free from handling money. When my partner and I first started our mountain shop, which sells white-water equipment, one of our part-time helpers used to find dollar bills and odds and ends of change lying around the store on boxes, on top of packs, or forgotten on shelves. The money was from merchandise I had sold to customers, and I absent-mindedly had gone on to help other people, not putting it in our money box. After I tell members of my party that story, I usually do not have to worry anymore about collecting group money. Someone always readily volunteers.

It is a good idea to collect a deposit early in the planning process. The deposit will give you a good idea of how many people are going on the trip so that boats may be reserved and lists of the members of the party can be sent to governmental agencies in charge of the river if they require it. When people put money down on something, it makes their commitment more serious.

The Group

For multi-day trips the number of people who are planning to go on your trip probably will change. I have seen trips change several times the month before we left. If it becomes a major problem, you may want to make the deposit nonrefundable. Even with such a deposit, however, you still need to make your initial plans flexible to adjust for a different-sized group when you finally take off on the trip. Vacation schedules change, someone may get ill before the trip begins, and a whole host of other problems can completely alter lists of parties. If you find that an agency managing the river you wish to run requires complete group lists months in advance, as some do, it is a good chance for you to write and provide input in the way rivers are managed. This is one regulation that is a hardship on noncommercial river runners, and if river managers are going to make any changes, they will have to hear from the users.

Main Group-Planning Session

At some time, you have to get the final group together before the beginning of the trip. Because of the changes that can occur in groups, you may want to have the group meeting a week, or as early as two to three days, before the departure date of the trip. With a meeting close to the time you plan to leave, you will be sure of exactly how many are going. If members of the party are coming in from out of town, this late meeting date will allow them to be involved in the planning. At this meeting, you can divvy up the responsibilities of getting the final things ready for the trip. The following are some aspects to consider at this meeting.

Food. Buying food for multi-day trips can be done in several ways:
- Everyone can bring his own food and do his own cooking. This method usually is utilized by two- to three-member parties, in which one stove or one fire can be shared as each person cooks his own meal. With larger groups, food usually is bought collectively.
- One or more members of the group can volunteer to do all the menu planning and go out and buy the food.
- Another way is to divide into cooking groups of two. Each cooking group plans one or more days of meals. They buy the food and prepare their meals on the river. In this way everyone in the party helps with meal planning, food buying, and cooking.

Collecting Money. At your last meeting, collect the rest of the money. Some of it then can be given to people who are buying food and the rest can be put in traveler's checks for paying gas expenses to and from the river.

Personal Equipment. With the party, go over a list of personal equipment and be sure everyone has adequate equipment and clothing for the trip (see the "Day and Overnight Equipment" chapter and

Pre-trip grocery shopping

"Checklists" at the end of the book).

Expectations and Safety. From the very beginning it is important that everyone in the group knows that he is expected to help in all the duties that are necessary in conducting a river trip. Fires need to be built, boats loaded and unloaded, campsites picked up, and so on. When everyone helps, the trip runs more smoothly and everyone has more leisure time. All party members also should realize before they go on the trip that there are potential dangers involved in white water. From a legal standpoint as well as a moral one, you and other knowledgeable people going on the trip should not create a false impression of the trip, making it sound like it is free from all dangers. Be objective and honest in your evaluation of what dangers are involved (see the chapter about hazards and safety).

After a quick review of the dangers, stress the importance of safety on the trip. A trip is only as safe as all the individual members make it. Everyone has a personal responsibility of doing his utmost to be safe.

Environment. At this meeting, remind people of the appropriate techniques to minimize environmental impact (see the chapter about camping). Explain the use of fire pans to prevent damage to campsites. You may follow a special procedure of handling human waste. Remind people not to put soaps in wild, unpolluted rivers. These procedures and others are essential to keeping users from destroying the river environment.

Leadership

On river trips with guides, it is fairly straightforward as to who is in the leadership position—the guides. On noncommercial trips—the type of trip this book is all about—there may be a designated leader, but more often than not, a democratic leadership develops. Leadership among equally experienced boaters is shared. The various decisions are made democratically by expressing differing opinions in front of the group so that everyone understands. In certain situations where the group has to make important decisions, such as whether or not to put in a river in high flows, inexperienced people should give more weight to the opinions of the more experienced boaters in the group. Democracy on river trips works well as long as people maintain an easy-going attitude and are willing to give and take. This way of approaching leadership allows personal freedom in a sport that, by its own nature, essentially is free.

Transportation

If you are planning a lightweight-style trip, transporting equipment does not present too many problems. For luxurious-style trips, however, getting to and from the river can be a major undertaking. Different means are available:

- Cartop carriers normally carry kayaks and canoes, but a good sturdy model also can be used for carrying oars, paddles, boat frames, and odds and ends of gear.
- Pickup trucks, vans, and Travel-Alls are handy for carrying gear. Be careful not to load vehicles past their recommended allowance. We did that to a pickup once and it burned a quart

of oil every fifty miles. By the time we coaxed it back home, the engine was ready for a major overhaul.

- Trailers can be rented or borrowed and are especially helpful for carrying bulky boats and frames to the river.

On luxurious trips where personal vehicles are subjected to much wear and tear, you may want to consider reimbursing some amount per mile to the vehicles' owners. It seems that if anything can go wrong on a river trip, it invariably goes wrong with the vehicles. Good procedures dictate caravaning in case problems develop. On one trip I did last summer, none of the three vehicles was together while traveling home from the river. The pickup truck in which I was riding carried most of the group gear and towed a large trailer, full of kayaks. Approximately 250 miles from home, the transmission went out on the truck and we were left stranded along the highway without the rest of our party to help. As it was, we were lucky to find someone to lock up our gear in a garage while the vehicle was repaired in a nearby town. Driving a rented car, we were nearly 100 miles from home when we noticed a deserted vehicle parked off the side of the road. As it seemed vaguely familiar, we stopped to take a closer look. It was one of the other vehicles from our trip, which we found out later also had broken down and left the vehicle's occupants stranded. For that trip, the score was two out of three vehicles broken down. The following week while some friends were on a river trip, all three of their vehicles broke down.

One last comment about traveling: Be sure everyone knows where you are going. Some other boating friends drove off one weekend to run a desert river. The put-in was located somewhere out in a maze of roads crisscrossing the desert. The two vehicles they drove became separated and finally, in exhaustion, one of the groups stopped to get some sleep. The problem was that their sleeping bags were carried in the other vehicle. To make it through the chilly desert night, one fellow curled up in the cramped Volkswagen and another climbed into the canvas bag that carried the rubber raft. They never found the river and finally returned home, much to their chagrin and the amusement of their friends back home.

Sometimes reliable, sometimes unreliable, river trip transportation

Solo Boating

By far the safest situation on a river trip is going with two or more people. On some difficult rivers, it is better to organize a party of at least four or five boaters so you have extra people to help if you run into problems. It is particularly important to adhere to this general rule when you are beginning and learning about white water.

Occasionally, some people will boat rivers alone. It goes against what most books advise, but I feel strongly that a person with many rivers and many days of experience under his belt can have rich and rewarding experiences boating alone. (One of the best personal descriptions I have read of solo kayaking is contained in *Does the Wet Suit You?*, Whit Deschner's small, richly illustrated book, listed in the "Books" section of the "Sources" chapter.) There is no doubt that solo boating is not so safe as boating with others, and thus the person who ponders boating alone must fully understand that he is greatly increasing the risks. If he makes the choice, he should never expect a rescue if he runs into trouble. If the solo boater finds himself injured, there is little chance of help anyway. It is this additional risk that makes the solo trip a magnificent experience, yet in the case of an accident, a grim defeat.

I have boated alone on Alaskan and Canadian rivers. Scenes come to mind of paddling to shore, seeing fresh grizzly bear and wolf tracks. One time I kayaked alone on a river in the southwestern United States. Along one stretch in the early morning, a snowy egret repeatedly landed and flew in front of me for numerous miles. When I finally stopped to stretch out on the sun-baked sand near where I had last seen the egret, I found a falls of crystal water falling free from a cliff above the river. A slight breeze blew a veil of water across the deep blue of the sky, creating a rainbow against it.

Somewhere along a river . . .
another magical place

RIVER CUISINE

On my first river trips—and on a few since—buying food was fairly easy: run a cart down the aisle of a grocery store; throw in noodles, rice, cheese, salami, oatmeal, and other items; toss the grocery sack in the back seat of the car; and leave for the river.

The food selection was particularly limited on one trip. Every morning we boiled up Maypo. Every lunch we ate crackers, cheese, and salami. And every dinner we consumed a Lipton dinner. After several days, the Lipton dinners, which are various processed noodle dishes to which boiling water is added, began tasting like the boxes in which they were packed. Every morning it became harder to spoon the heavy, sticky Maypo out of the cup into the mouth. That ended it for me. Since that trip, I have never been able to eat Maypo or Lipton dinners.

Then someone who was a little better organized and had more refined culinary skills than I brought along a Dutch oven and purchased fresh vegetables, fruits, and meats. Meals changed from Lipton dinners to chicken and broccoli, enchiladas, and tasty stews. On each succeeding trip, someone came up with a new mouth-watering dish to drive boating mates into a gastronomic frenzy.

For those of us who were used to mere backpacking food, Dutch oven cuisine was a pleasant change. Had I been a purist, seeking to meet nature in its simplest and rawest of terms, I would not have indulged in such decadence on a white-water river. Fortunately, I was not a purist and felt no pangs of guilt while feeding on the culinary delights that the Dutch oven and fresh food provided.

Even if you are on a self-contained kayak trip, or on any other kind of white-water trip in which lightness is essential, and you must forgo fresh foods and Dutch ovens, delicious and nutritious meals can be made if you use a little forethought. In this chapter we will take a look at eating well— on lightweight as well as heavyweight trips.

River Cookery Styles

A *lightweight* style of cooking is utilized by self-contained kayakers, or canoeists and rafters who wish to travel as light as possible. They carry the same types of food that a backpacker uses and prepare the food in aluminum pots heated by small backpacking stoves or, if it is environmentally acceptable, campfires.

A *luxurious* style of cooking can be utilized by those traveling with

Lightweight stove and cooking
gear on an early season
multi-day kayak trip

rafts that can carry the extra weight. Iced coolers keep vegetables and meats fresh, and cast-iron cookware and all sorts of pots, pans, and kitchen utensils are available for food preparation.

A boater, of course, can choose any style to his liking within these extremes.

Developing Menus

To help make the food buying go a little smoother, make a list of food that will be needed on the trip. If making lists is a little too organized for your style, use my method of devising a menu—while pushing a cart down the aisle of a grocery store. Normally, however, the more organized approaches yield better meals.

I do not think it is necessary to sit down and figure the calorie and mineral content of the meals. Use the same common sense that you

Getting organized

incorporate in your home menu planning. One hint that will help is to plan a wide variety of food items for each meal. For instance, for a lightweight lunch, instead of having just crackers and cheese, bring salami, nuts, raisins, jerky, dried fruits, and some candy to give the lunch a little more pizzazz. Remember, appetites are greater when you are out in fresh air and exercising, and you will want to bring larger meals than you plan at home. Whether you are traveling light or in luxury, always keep some snack food in an easy-to-get-to place. Snacking throughout the day helps keep everyone energized and is especially essential on cold days to help ward off hypothermia.

Lightweight Breakfasts

Whether it is a chilly trip on a Labrador river or a blustery, sunny week on a desert river in Arizona, a hot drink such as tea, instant coffee, hot chocolate, or hot Jell-O is a nice way of starting breakfast. Then have the main meal be any of the following:

    Instant hot cereals (Maypo, oatmeal, cream of wheat, etc.)

    Cold cereals (granola, Grape Nuts, etc.)

    Freeze-dried breakfasts (available at backpacking and outdoor stores)

    Snack foods that do not require cooking (cheese, crackers, salami, jerky, nuts, dried fruit, etc.)

    Leftovers from the previous night's supper

Lightweight Lunches

In order to save time, lunch typically is not cooked. A few boaters may schedule a special day on which they may cook a lunch, but this usually requires too much extra time for it to be done every day. It is, however, a good idea to bring some extra hot drinks or soup mixes for cold, rainy

days when a hot accompaniment to lunch is a welcome addition.
Some suggestions for a lightweight lunch include:
Salami
Canned fish (tuna, salmon, kippers, sardines, etc.)
Canned meat (sandwich spreads, chicken, beef, etc.)
Jerky
Crackers
Cheese
Dried fruits (raisins, apples, apricots, pears, etc.)
Various types of candies (sugar or honey)
Peanut butter
Granola
Nuts (cashews, Spanish, sunflower, etc.)
Gorp (mixtures of nuts, raisins, chocolate chips, etc.)

Lunch

Lightweight Suppers

Soup or hot drinks soon after arriving at the evening's campsite are a quick predinner warm-up. The main course can consist of freeze-dried dinners, the lightest and most convenient types of food available. The best types of freeze-dried dinners are those to which you add hot water, then wait just a few minutes before eating them. Unfortunately, the convenience of freeze-dried dinners comes with a correspondingly high price. You also can put together many fine, nutritional, lightweight meals by buying products at your local grocery store, where various types of dehydrated foods and "convenience" meals are available.

For simplicity, most lightweight meals are cooked in one pot, although some people prepare separate dishes in more than one pot. To help plan one-pot meals, see the "Lightweight One-Pot Suppers" chart. Start with one or more of the bases, then add one or more items from each of the other categories.

Lightweight One-Pot Suppers

Bases
Rice (brown, white, wild) Noodles (egg, wheat, spinach) Macaroni (egg, wheat, spinach) Spaghetti (egg or wheat) Instant soups Beans (pinto, red, kidney, etc.) Ramen noodles Bouillon cubes Canned tomato sauces, V-8 juice, etc. Powdered sauces (gravy mixes, tomato sauce mixes, etc.) Packaged "convenience" dinners (Hamburger Helper, Tuna Helper, etc.) Instant potatoes Other grains (bulgur, buckwheat, etc.)

Meats	Meat Substitutes	Vegetables	Toppings and Garnishes
Canned meats (beef, Spam, turkey, chicken, etc.) Canned seafood (tuna, bonita, sardines, shrimp, crab, oysters, clams, etc.) Freeze-dried meats Jerky Salami and sausage	Texturized vegetable protein and various types of packaged dried-meat substitutes Canned meat substitutes (beef, chicken, turkey, "vegie-links," etc.) Vegetable bacon bits Cheese	Freeze-dried or dehydrated vegetables (carrots, potatoes, corn, peas, etc.) Fresh or canned vegetables (potatoes, carrots, zucchini, etc.)	Seeds (sunflower, sesame, chia, etc.) Chopped nuts (walnuts, almonds, peanuts, etc.) Wheat germ Brewers' yeast Cheese

Luxurious-Style Breakfasts

As in lightweight breakfasts, a good warm-up for a luxurious breakfast is a hot drink. Prepare coffee, set a pot of water on the fire or stove, and lay out several different types of teas, hot chocolate, and/or Jell-O. Let members of the party help themselves while you prepare the main breakfast. Some parties like to mix up frozen fruit juices such as apple, orange, or grapefruit for an extra treat along with the main meal.

The main course can consist of those items suggested under "Lightweight Breakfasts" or such typical morning meals as:
Bacon and eggs
Pancakes
Omelets (vegetarian, Spanish, etc.)
Eggs (scrambled, fried, poached, etc.)
Fruit

Hashbrowns
Egg and potato casseroles
Quiches
French toast

Luxurious-Style Lunches

Since cooking is time-consuming while on the river most, if not all, lunches are served cold. Lunches may consist of the same items suggested under "Lightweight Lunches," or may include any of the following suggestions:

Bread
Rolls
Bagels
Lunch meats (turkey, beef, corned beef, bologna, etc.)
Salami or sausage
Cheese
Peanut butter
Jam
Pickles
Mayonnaise, mustard, catsup
Fresh fruit
Candy and cookies
Leftovers from previous day's breakfast or supper

Luxurious-Style Suppers

Just about anything goes for suppers on luxurious-style trips. With Dutch ovens, practically anything that you make at home can be made on the river. An excellent book, full of exotic Dutch oven meals, is Sheila Mills's *Rocky Mountain Kettle Cuisine* (see the "Books" section in the "Sources" chapter).

To warm up after a long chilly day on the river, or to quench ravenous hunger, start out with a soup. Use packaged mixes or canned soups, or even start from scratch. The primary course can center around meat such as steaks, hamburgers, pork chops, or chicken, or it can be vegetarian. Various salads (lettuce, fruit, bean, and potato) balance out the main meal. Bread or biscuits can be baked for a supplement and for a nightcap, dessert—including pies, cakes, brownies, or popcorn—are fun to make later in the evening when everyone is gathered around the evening fire. (For more information, see the "Dutch Oven Cookery" section later in this chapter.)

Natural Foods

Whole grains, food without preservatives, and organically grown food can be carried on river trips. For those traveling light, many types of organically grown dried vegetables and fruits are available at stores or you of course can bring along food that you have dried yourself. Dehydrated and freeze-dried organic meals are available at organic grocery stores. To provide quick energy on long days or to help prevent

Evening fare—enchiladas, salsa, guacamole, and nachos

hypothermia, you can eat honey-based cookies and candies instead of white sugar products. A fine book about preparing tasty, lightweight, meatless, sugarless, and chemical-free meals is Vikki Kinmont's and Claudia Axcell's *Simple Foods for the Pack* (see the "Books" section in the "Sources" chapter).

For luxurious-style trips, you can carry all types of fresh vegetables, fruits, and grains in order to create superb meals.

Vegetarian Cookery

Before planning meals, find out if any members of the party are vegetarians. Sometimes the entire group will enjoy a vegetarian diet for the trip. On other trips, however, the group may consist of a mixture of both meat-eaters and vegetarians. With forethought, meals can be planned with plenty of variety to keep both types of folks happy. For example, tacos make an adaptable supper. They are easily prepared and can include ground beef for the meat-eaters in addition to lettuce, grated cheese, sprouts, and chopped tomatoes, green onions, green peppers, and mushrooms. Any combination of these ingredients is wrapped in a tortilla. Served with corn tortilla chips with melted cheese on top, this simple dinner makes a fine filling dish for all.

Dutch Oven Cookery

If you have the craft and the load-carrying ability, Dutch ovens are a superb implement for preparing river meals. Most Dutch ovens are constructed of heavy cast iron and are available in various diameters and depths. To help save weight, though, cast aluminum models that perform well also are available. The size to bring on trips depends on the number of people in your group. A small party of two or three can get by with one ten- or twelve-inch Dutch oven, or perhaps two if they plan to bake breads with meals. Twelve-inch ovens serve a group of up to ten; larger groups need a fourteen-inch size.

Dutch oven epicurean delight

The following hints will help in using a Dutch oven.

Seasoning.   A Dutch oven that is "seasoned" well will perform well. A seasoned pot, in which oil has soaked into the pores of the cast metal, keeps food from sticking, helps distribute heat, and resists rusting. If a Dutch oven looks dry after storage, wipe the inside and outside with a little oil to give it a black, shiny look. New Dutch ovens can be seasoned by partially filling them with oil and heating them for several hours at a low heat in a home oven or over a fire.

Stews.   Thick, hearty stews with vegetables and/or meat are traditional on river trips. If you are using meat, brown it first in hot oil in the bottom of the Dutch oven. When the meat is brown, add water or tomato juice or various soup starters and the rest of the vegetables. Put the lid on the Dutch oven to hold in heat and adjust the coals so that the mixture bubbles just slightly.

Sautéing and Frying.   Vegetables can be sautéed easily in a Dutch oven. Pour in oil and allow it to get hot, then add whatever vegetables are desired, stirring and heating until they are done. Various vegetable dishes and many Chinese meals can be prepared in this manner.

Chicken, steaks, hamburgers, and other meats can be fried in a little oil in the bottom of a hot oven. One favorite on river trips is cheeseburgers with all the trimmings and French fries, deep-fried in an oven partially filled with oil.

Bulky Meats.   Turkey, prime rib, and other bulky meats also can be prepared in a Dutch oven. If yours is not deep enough or wide enough, cut the meat or poultry into large pieces. Place the lid on the Dutch oven and heat it with coals on the top and bottom. On a kayak workshop I organize each summer, we take off two days to do a backpacking trip. The people who decide to stay in camp while the others go backpacking cook a turkey. Upon returning from the hike, we all join together for a turkey dinner with dressing, mashed potatoes, gravy, vegetables, and dessert— decadence at its best.

Baking.   With a Dutch oven, you can bake breads, biscuits, cakes, brownies, pies, quiches, and other goodies. You will need coals for baking. If it is environmentally acceptable, build a fire in a fire pan and scoop out the coals with a shovel. In areas where fires are not permitted or are not desirable, bring along charcoal briquettes. Putting a number of briquettes underneath and on top of the oven works well for baking.

While you prepare the ingredients, heat the oven and its lid. When you are ready, wipe the oven with oil and pour in the ingredients.

If you are cooking over a fire, it is best to keep the oven away from the main part of the fire. Bring a separate small fire pan (a garbage can lid or upside-down metal bucket will suffice). Place some coals on the fire pan, set the oven on it, and place more coals on top of the lid. Concentrate the heat on top of the oven by placing twice as many coals on top as on the bottom. To help provide even heat, rotate the oven and its lid every so often.

Placing coals on Dutch oven lid for baking

Packing Food

Food for lightweight trips can be packed in plastic bags and further protected by placing all food items in one or more burlap bags or nylon stuff bags (available at backpacking stores).

On luxurious trips, many of the fresh foods have to be carried in coolers. A major cause of spoilage occurs when ice in coolers melts, dampening food items. To eliminate this problem, freeze water in plastic containers, such as plastic milk or soft drink containers, several days before the trip. When the ice melts, the food will stay dry and the water in the container can be used for drinking.

Keeping meat from spoiling is a special problem on longer trips in hot weather. One solution is to have the meat frozen several days before you leave. On the departure day, buy dry ice and place it in the cooler with a couple of frozen plastic containers of water. The dry ice will sublimate in a day, but the ice in the water containers still will be frozen and, if you are careful, will continue to keep the meat cool for a week, and sometimes longer.

The less often coolers are open, the better. Develop a system in which all the items for the last meals of the trip are in one cooler. Tape the cooler shut with duct tape and do not open it until you need to prepare the last meals of the trip.

After packing coolers and other containers of food, write down their contents on the tops. For instance, on one cooler, you might write: "Monday and Tuesday breakfasts—eggs, cheese, green peppers,

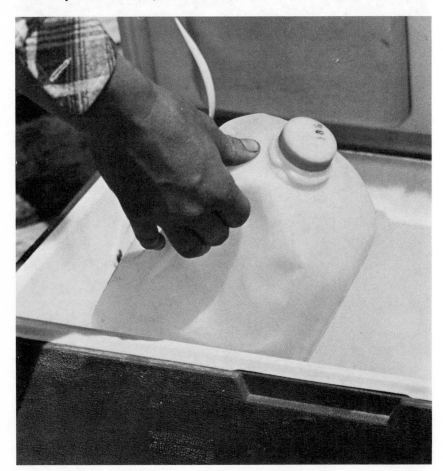

Frozen water in plastic containers prevents melt water from soaking and spoiling contents of coolers, and the melt water can be used for drinking.

Labeled food containers eliminate the frustrating search through many containers to find one item.

onions, frozen orange juice." This saves having to look through all the containers to find one item that you may need to prepare a meal.

Items such as tea, coffee, oil, paper towels, seasonings, and so on can be packed together in one bag if they are used for every meal.

On hot days when you are concerned about food spoilage, try to tie up the boat in shady areas. Covering food containers with white tarps, kept damp throughout the day, will help keep the food cool.

CAMPING AND LESSENING ENVIRONMENTAL IMPACT

I paddled my kayak to a sandy beach on the right shore of the North Fork of the Fortymile River in Alaska. The site looked fine for a camp and I slowly climbed out of the confining seat. At one end of the beach I erected my small A-frame tent. Far away on the other end, in order to keep food-sniffing bears away from my sleeping quarters, I built a cooking fire.

Near the Arctic Circle, the Fortymile's summer is not darkened by night. Rather, following a long crimson sunset, a twilight illuminates the lonely land of stunted white and black spruce growing above the flowery tundra. I sat for hours resting my back against the pack watching the fire of the setting sun dancing on the rippling waters of the river.

Later, I hung the food bag in a slender tree that probably would pose little problem to a hungry bear, but at least provided me with some psychological assurance, and I dragged the boat and gear above the tent. Sleep came easily.

The sun had risen when I was awakened by a movement close to my head. The side of the tent pushed toward me and then fell back, then pushed forward again. This time the cool, moist nylon material pushed against my face. Suddenly realizing what was happening, I sprang out of my bag.

Outside, only a three-foot-wide strip of beach remained where it once had been fifty feet wide. During the night the river had risen over a vertical yard. I scampered around, stark naked, throwing things out of the tent to higher ground before the waves washed inside and wet my sleeping bag and clothing. I toppled the tent and watched as the rest of the beach slowly was inundated.

Fortunately, I had expected high water because it had rained hard the previous day, and so had moved the kayak and gear to high ground. If I had not, the rising river would have washed it away, leaving me with the prospects of a long, arduous journey through the Alaskan wilderness without vital survival equipment. As I dramatically learned from the experience, it does not hurt to be cautious when it is raining.

Besides rain, a number of other things should be considered when river camping. We will take a closer look at them in this chapter. White-water rivers are a premium resource and because of their popularity, those rivers on which overnight or multi-day trips occur are subjected to intense environmental pressures at the campsites. Only so many campsites are located on a river, and those are used day in and day out all during the season. Therefore, it is vital that river runners utilize camping procedures that minimize their impact on the environment so that those who follow also will have a pristine river experience. As we consider the aspects of river camping in this chapter, we will look at how we can leave no traces of ourselves.

Choosing a Campsite

Start looking for a campsite well before it gets dark. On one trip I was on, darkness forced us to camp in a canyon with no available flat areas. After cooking dinner in a boulder field, some of the party slept in boats and the others rigged up a three-hundred-foot handline to reach two small, tilted benches perched on the hillside above the river.

On some rivers the land agency managing the area may assign campsites, while on others, the choice of a campsite is up to you. In areas where mosquitoes, no-see-ums, and other pests are a problem, beaches and gravel bars are preferable to heavily infested grassy and vegetated areas. Beach and gravel bar campsites also are better choices since environmental damage can be kept to a minimum. Grassy areas, if heavily used, become trampled and gradually lose their vegetation as boaters pass back and forth. If it is necessary to sleep in a grassy or vegetated area, try to do the cooking where most campsite activity takes place—on rocks on the shore of the river or at the edge of the grass—so the area will not be damaged.

Gravel bars with a coarse covering of river rocks at first seem inhospitable places for erecting a tent and sleeping. Often, however, the slight inconvenience is well worth getting away from bugs and having an open, aesthetically pleasing camp. Thick foam pads or a couple of Ensolite pads placed on top of each other will cushion the rocks for more comfortable sleeping. Tents can be staked out by placing the tent stakes horizontally in the loop and covering them with rocks or wedging them between rocks to keep them secure.

Tents and tarps can be staked on gravel bars by wedging lines tied to sticks between rocks.

Sandy beaches work well for camping. The place where you sleep can be conformed comfortably to your back by scooping out a little sand in the buttocks area. Remember, though, that beaches and gravel bars were formed by the river in a higher water stage. If it is pouring rain, or you are located on a desert flash flood river, be sure that you have an escape route to higher ground behind the campsite. If low ground exists between you and the shore, the high river may create a new channel, blocking access.

Occasionally in bad weather or in windy conditions, you may want to find more protected areas in brush- or tree-covered camps. If you have a choice of sites, you also may want to consider if the area has a swimming hole, shade in hot weather, sunshine in the morning, a pile of driftwood for a fire, a good wave by the campsite for kayak surfing, and/or good fishing.

Securing Boats

To secure a kayak for the night, drag it up on shore, jam the paddle inside the boat, and place rocks on wet suits, flotation bags, and other gear in case the wind comes up. I have seen unprotected paddles blown off the beach into the river.

After rafts have been unpacked, pull them up on shore and tie them to a tree or large boulder as an extra precaution.

Some rivers on which flows are controlled by a dam have fluctuating water levels. If the level fluctuates greatly, you may want to wake up every so often during the night in order to push or pull the boat on or off the beach according to high or low fluctuations.

One thing to watch out for when tying up rafts is abrasion. In waves, a raft can vibrate back and forth against a rock and wear a hole through the material. If your boat is parked in an area where waves are affecting it, pull it far enough up on shore to stop the movement.

Shelter

If the weather is threatening or the wind is gusty, set up your tent or tarp behind some type of windbreak, such as bushes, trees, and/or large

Rafts should be secured to prevent them from washing away due to wave action or a rise in water level.

boulders. Otherwise, any flat area is fine. If the night is clear and no bugs are out, you may want to sleep outside under the stars.

Tarps can be tied to trees, bushes, and boulders to form a lean-to. If no natural tie-on points are available, oars or paddles can be lashed together to form a tripod to which the tarp can be tied. Or the four corners of the tarp can be staked out and a stick used as a center pole. In rain, a tarp erected near the fire will be welcomed by those preparing and cooking the meal.

Woodsmen of the past dug trenches around their tents and tarps to prevent water from pooling. A small, hand-scooped trench on a sandy beach does not hurt anything, but trenches dug in vegetated or grassy areas or in solid earth are extremely damaging and should be avoided. If pooling of water might be a problem, simply choose areas on a slight incline or away from depressions where water collects. Obviously, pine bow beds for camping also are something to let rest in woodsmen history.

Fires and Fire Pans

While some members of the party are setting up tarps, others can get the stove or fire going and the cooking underway. Before leaving on a trip you will need to decide whether to use a stove or to build fires. In some popular areas where there is little driftwood and the riverside has been scoured for wood—trees chopped down and all branches of standing timber broken off within arm's reach—stoves are a must. In other areas where driftwood is plentiful, a fire is acceptable, but use only driftwood and downed, dead trees. Breaking branches off trees leaves unsightly, broken stumps and increases the possibility of disease. To ensure an evening's wood supply, pick up driftwood along the river before reaching camp.

Stoves should be used in areas in which campfires are environmentally destructive.

If you plan to build fires, seriously consider bringing fire pans if they are not already required by the land management agency. A fire pan is the best way to contain ashes and prevent fire scars in campsites. If you have a party of rafts, carrying a fire pan is not difficult. Self-contained kayakers can use hub caps or oil pans. On infrequently run rivers, having a fire without a fire pan will cause little harm as long as the fire area is thoroughly cleaned up after use. On popular rivers, however, self-contained kayakers should plan to cook on backpacking stoves and wear warm wet suits so they do not have to use warming fires.

Set up the fire pan on rocks to hold it off the ground so it does not scorch the substrate and destroy soil microorganisms. The first evening of the trip, place a thin layer of sand or dirt in the bottom of the pan to keep the fire from burning through. On some rivers, the ashes can be disposed of the next day by dumping them in the middle of the river in strong current. Sue Villard, who for several years worked for the Forest Service on the Middle Fork of Idaho's Salmon River, said that few people ever dumped ashes into the current properly. Most boaters simply dumped them in the eddy by camp, so the ashes eventually washed back on shore, dirtying the beaches. To prevent problems such as these, all kayak groups should dump ashes along the shore at a place where the current is strong and will wash them downstream. Rafters should put ashes in bailing buckets and wait to dump them until they are underway in the strong current in the middle of the river.

On clean or nearly clean rivers in wild areas, it is best to store the

Before using a fire pan, add a thin layer of sand or ashes saved from the previous night's camp.

Storing ashes to be used as a covering on the bottom of the fire pan at the next night's camp. In this way, ashes can be carried from camp to camp and off the river, keeping campsites and beaches clean.

ashes in an ammo can and carry them out. To prepare the ashes for storage, moisten them until they are cool and shovel them into the ammo can. At the next camp, dump the ashes out of the ammo can into the fire pan before starting the fire. As the ashes are used again and again at each camp, they gradually are reduced to a fine dust as the trip progresses. One hint in carrying out ashes is to use predominantly small sticks for fuel in the fire, especially in the morning fire. The smaller sticks burn hot and break down into small ashes, while larger logs burn slowly and sometimes never burn completely.

Try not to spill coals, but if you do, pick them up. If possible, locate the fire pan near the river, so high water can clean away any coals that accidentally are dropped. Use a fire pan with at least five-inch sides to minimize the spilling of coals. Some campsites and sandy beaches on popular rivers are becoming so littered with ashes that the soil or sand is turning black. Think of the campsite as your home and any coals that drop as falling on your carpet. Steve Carothers of the Museum of Northern Arizona (in Flagstaff) has conducted research on minimizing environmental impact on rivers. He suggests an additional safety tip about removing fire pans. Throw a little water on the ground as soon as the pan is removed because even when the pan is elevated, the ground below it still is very hot and can burn party members who have bare feet.

If possible, set up fire pans near the river. Any small pieces of ashes that are accidentally missed when cleaning up in the morning will be washed out by high water.

Fires without Pans

If you must build a fire without a fire pan, build it below the high-water mark on the rocky shoreline, in gravel, or in a bare place where it is easy to destroy and remove all remains. If the fire is below the high-water mark, any coals that accidentally are left will be washed out by higher flows.

Carothers reminds boaters to build small fires. An entire meal for a small party can be cooked with a couple handfuls of small sticks.

When you are finished with the fire, thoroughly douse it with water and, as much as possible, restore the site to normal. Throw any blackened rocks in the river. Even on remote rivers in northwestern Canada, I always have destroyed any sign of my fires.

One of the most atrocious scars left by campers are large blackened boulders against which a fire has been built. Always avoid building fires with or without fire pans near any large boulders, against a cliff, or in a cave.

Fire Hazards

In dry areas in fire season, some land management agencies may require you to use stoves. It is a good idea to give the agency a call before leaving on a trip if fire conditions look touchy.

While camping, do not build a fire near dry grass, pine needles, brush, or tree branches overhead. When wood or grass is dry, it is shocking how fast a fire can flare up and spread before anything can be done to stop it. On a trip on a desert river, one person in the party before us accidentally started a fire when burning toilet paper. A gust of wind spread the fire over several acres in no time. Another party stopped to help, and the more than thirty people were barely enough to put it out.

It is a good idea to keep a couple of bailing buckets full of water near the fire. Someone also should be with the fire at all times and the fire should be doused before retiring to bed. If you build a fire without a fire pan, be sure it is built on mineral soil and not in the decaying, vegetative matter. Fires can burn underground in vegetative matter for days, then suddenly flame up into a fire. A number of large destructive fires have been started in this way.

Cooking Precautions

River running is a famous activity for picking up intestinal bugs. One of the most obvious precautions for preventing health problems—though it often is forgotten by boaters—is for those helping with the cooking to wash their hands.

Another precaution is to clean the knives used in preparing food. Everyday uses of sheath knives and jack knives can contaminate the blades and hinges. Some river runners bring along extra knives for cooking, which is convenient but not always practical. To sterilize a knife before cutting food, wash it and pass it through an open flame, or better yet, throw it in a pot of boiling water for a few minutes.

If you are cooking with a Dutch oven, use a pair of gloves and pliers for holders to help prevent burns, a frequent injury among river runners.

Drinking Water

On the great majority of rivers, water must be boiled or treated before it is fit to drink. At camp at night is a good time to prepare water. Vigorously boil it for ten minutes, then pour it back and forth between a couple of pots to reaerate it. This is the best method of purification, but it results in purified water that tastes bad. One of the best purification methods, resulting in more palatable water, is to use iodine. According to the directions of Fredrick Kahn and Barbara Visscher in an article in *The Western Journal of Medicine* (May 1975), add a couple of grams of USP-grade resublimed iodine (available at a pharmacy with a doctor's

One of the pleasures of white-water boating is running a river in which the water is clear and pure enough to drink. Unfortunately, such rivers are few.

prescription) to a one-ounce clear-glass bottle that has a lid that will not leak. Fill the bottle with water and shake it for about a minute. Then allow the crystals of iodine to settle to the bottom. What you now have is essentially a saturated solution of iodine that can be used to disinfect water. *Pour off the iodine solution, not the crystals.* The crystals are left in the bottle to make more iodine solution. For a quart of cold water around the freezing point, use about eight capfuls (assuming that a capful of a typical one-ounce bottle is approximately 2.5 cubic centimeters); for warmer water, use about five capfuls. The iodine crystals can be used hundreds of times over an unlimited amount of time without replenishing them. After treating water, pour it into your various plastic water containers.

Showering

Unless river regulations require an alternative procedure, do all personal washing above the high-water mark, being sure that none of the waste water runs into the river or side streams. *Never put soap in side streams or in the river.* There are two methods of getting spruced up. In the *sponge method*, first fill a helmet, bailing bucket, or cooking pot with water. Wet a washcloth or handkerchief and wash yourself, replacing the water as need be. Do not throw the used water back into the river, but rather onto shore, above the high-water mark.

The *shower method* is best done with the help of a friend. Strip down, jump into the river to get wet, and walk up to a point above the high-water mark. If the shore is rocky, wear tennis shoes to protect your feet. Soap up using a biodegradable soap sparingly. Meanwhile, your friend fills a bucket, a large pot, or a storage flotation bag with water and walks up to where you are. He then slowly dumps the water on you while you rinse off. It is great fun and a refreshing way of getting cleaned up.

Garbage

If you do not have an open fire, place refuse—including organic garbage—in plastic bags, then in a burlap bag (to contain any spills), and carry it out. Organic garbage, including leftover food, orange peels, fish entrails, apple cores, and so on, attracts flies and the same types of pests that are found in a city dump. Even buried organic waste can be dug up by animals and strewed about. If for some reason you cannot carry out organic garbage, at least bury it far away from the river and campsite. Be careful to pack down the dirt and replace the sod over the hole afterward so no sign of it remains.

Cans, bottles, and plastic never should be left or buried. If these items are carried in, they must be carried out. On some rivers where outhouses are available at campsites, be sure no one in the party throws any of the group's garbage, especially plastic bags and cans, in the toilet pit. Besides filling up the outhouse sooner than necessary, the plastic

Garbage should be removed from the river.

To cut down on garbage volume, tin cans can be smashed and flattened.

prevents normal decomposition of feces and may prevent that site from ever being available for another outhouse. When sites are exhausted, river runners may be required to bring in portable toilets to carry out human waste.

If you have a fire, you can burn organic garbage. Build up the fire with small sticks to get it hot, then scatter garbage on the fire in a thin layer. Allow the fire to consume it, build up the fire again, spread on more garbage, and so on until all the garbage is burned. If you have a lot of wet garbage, it is best to carry it out since burning it wastes a lot of wood and takes a long time.

Tin cans can be burned to clean out the insides, but after burning them, smash them and carry them out in a plastic garbage bag.

Avoid throwing aluminum in the fire. Various items such as beer and pop cans, cocoa packages, cigarette packages, and the lining of some food containers are made of aluminum. It does not burn completely in the fire, and wind can scatter unsightly pieces around the area. Instead, put all aluminum foil and cans in a separate bag and drop it off at a recycling center on the way home.

Dishwashing

If you are cooking with a backpacking stove and pot and eating with a cup and spoon, washing is a simple procedure. Be sure, however, to wash away from the river so no waste water drains into it.

On luxurious trips with numerous plates, cups, silverware, and pots, the best procedure is to set up a three-bucket wash. In the first bucket add very hot water with some biodegradable dishwashing soap. Use the second bucket for rinsing and the third bucket, with a capful of Clorox in it, for disinfecting dishes. It seems like an involved way of washing, but it actually works quickly and prevents intestinal problems that occur from using contaminated dishes.

Do not wash Dutch ovens in soap, which can ruin their seasoning. Instead, scrape out the leftover food and add water, heating it slowly over the fire or coals. Stir the water until the Dutch oven is clean, then wipe oil on the inside until the oven takes on a shiny appearance.

Never dispose of dishwater, leftover food, or soap in side streams or the main river unless advised otherwise by the managing agency of the river. On a few rivers such as the Colorado, there is less environmental impact if the dishwater first is strained of any solid food particles or coffee grounds, then is disposed of in the main current (not in eddies) rather than on land. *Use this procedure, however, only on rivers where it is specifically recommended.* On other rivers, the best disposal method is to dig a hole, carefully removing sod. Use this same hole for draining dishwater throughout the time you are camped at a campsite. The hole should be away from the camp and above the high-water mark of the river. When you are ready to leave, fill in the hole, pack down the soil, and replace the sod so that it is not distinguishable.

Human Waste

Another major environmental problem on rivers is human waste. On rivers where there are no regulations concerning human waste, always

The three-bucket wash

urinate or defecate above the high-water mark. When defecating, each person in a small group should use a shovel or small garden trowel to dig a hole not more than ten inches deep. It is in the top layers of soil that decomposition takes place at the most rapid rate. For those who have open fires, toilet paper can be burned in the fire. Otherwise, place it in a plastic bag and carry it out in the garbage. Some people burn their toilet paper on the site, but do so only in a fail-safe place. Numerous forest fires have been started by people burning toilet paper, so it usually is best to carry it out.

If you find yourself in a situation where it is impossible to burn the paper or to carry it out, spread out the paper and mix it in with the feces with a stick. Cover the feces-paper mixture with soil, which will help the paper decompose faster. On any outdoor trip, bring the cheapest, undyed toilet paper money can buy because it decomposes more rapidly than other types.

For larger groups of twelve or more, dig one central latrine for everyone to use. Leave a bag, held down with a rock, near the latrine in which people can dispose of toilet paper. Before leaving, cover the hole, carefully replace the sod, and burn the bag or throw it in the garbage.

Portable Toilets. Portable toilets are required on some rivers where human waste problems are severe. At first it sounds like an unpleasant hassle, but with a little practice you will find that it does not require much additional effort. Portable toilets and containers can be purchased at motor home and camper supply houses, or a simple one can be constructed easily out of large ammo cans. The "Carothers's Crapper," as it is called after Steve Carothers, who advocated its use after his intensive research on environmental problems of river campers on the Colorado River, is made by lining a large ammo can (11 by 12 by 5½ inches or an equivalent size) with a heavy-duty plastic garbage bag. Two other garbage bags are placed through the hole of a toilet seat (available at camper or plumbing supply stores) and wrapped around it. Formaldehyde or lye is added to stop the biological production of methane.

Toilet paper is stored in a separate plastic bag, while used sanitary napkins, tampons, and so on, are placed in the toilet. Before leaving in the morning, the two plastic bags holding the feces are tied off and placed in

Digging a latrine

A portable toilet made from a large ammo can, toilet seat, and garbage bags

a third bag with the used toilet paper bag, and shut in the ammo can.

Carothers has found that an ammo can that is 18¾ by 14½ by 8⅛ inches can contain sixty to seventy-five man-days of feces, or in other words, it is sufficient for fifteen people on a five-day trip.

Sleeping on Cold Trips

If you are running rivers during winter or in cold parts of the year, be sure to bring enough warm clothing. At night, for warmth, use a sleeping pad under the sleeping bag. Air mattresses are not so warm as thick foam pads or doubled-up closed-cell foam pads such as Ensolite and blue foam. If you are chilly in a sleeping bag, you can gain extra insulation by wearing clothing in bed. On some trips, we have wrapped hot rocks, heated in the fire, in clothing to provide a little extra heat for those in cold sleeping bags. Be sure, however, that a rock is not so hot that it can burn or singe the clothing it is wrapped in.

Morning

In the morning, one of the early risers can get the fire or stove going to heat water for hot drinks. If you use a fire pan, keep the fire burning so ashes are reduced down in size for storage in the ammo can.

Before leaving, always scan the campsite for bits of paper or other rubbish. Food scraps from camping or lunches attract mice, flies, ants, bees, and other undesirables. Be sure all coals spilled from the fire pan have been picked up. Clean up any untidy messes left by careless campers before you. I sometimes even brush the ground with a piece of brush, and scatter leaves around to restore the campsite to as nearly a natural state as possible.

Hot Springs and Saunas

An added luxury on some rivers are hot springs where you can lie

Setting up a sauna

back and warm tired muscles. Remember not to use soap in a hot spring. For personal washing, use a bucket or a helmet to scoop out some water and wash a distance away from the spring so waste water will not drain back in.

Lacking a hot spring, you can construct a sauna for an exhilarating treat while on a river trip. A sandy beach is the best place, but practically any location along the river will suffice. Stake down all four corners of a tarp and use a stick in the middle as a center pole. Hold down the edges of the tarp with sand or rocks to keep steam from escaping, leaving one side of the tarp open so participants can get in and out.

Heat smooth, hard rocks in the fire for an hour or so. Stay away from glassy, volcanic rocks, limestone, and brittle rocks, which can explode. Place hot rocks inside cooking pots and carry them with pliers or gloves under the tarp. While everyone strips down and sits under the tarp, sprinkle water on the rocks to create steam. It is a good idea to keep a lid over the rocks just in case one might crack.

For the grand finale, take a dunk in the river, wearing tennis shoes if the shore is rocky. For many, the river sauna may be the highlight of their trip.

An evening sauna—a relaxing end to a day on the river

Last camp

CHECKLISTS

The following lists are suggestions. The actual equipment that you carry will depend on your likes and dislikes. The lists include most of the items that might be carried on a *luxurious* trip. If you plan to shave off pounds and have a lightweight-style trip, simply choose those items that will meet your needs yet still enable you to be safe and self-sufficient. These lists are designed so you can photocopy them and check off items when you are getting ready for trips.

Rafting

Boats and Accessories

☐ Inflatable raft and various parts (thwarts, bow and stern lines, boat bag, etc.)

☐ Frame, if used, and straps or cord for lashing frame to boat

☐ Oar boat: oars, oar stops, oarlocks or thole pins and clips, extra oars in addition to oarlocks

☐ Paddle boat: paddles for everyone, plus a couple of extras

☐ Pump

☐ Waterproof bags and/or rigid containers to carry gear and food

☐ Bailing buckets

☐ Straps, cord, carabiners, or clips for lashing gear above floor of boat

☐ Tarp to cover equipment on boat

Repair Kit

☐ Duct tape

☐ Patching material, glue, glue solvent (all of these items should be compatible with materials used in your raft)

☐ Scissors to cut material

☐ Brush to apply glue

☐ Sandpaper

☐ Rag

☐ Carpet thread or dental floss, and carpet needle to mend bad tears (some boaters use sewing awls)

Boat with a frame also would include:

☐ Tools (vise grips, pliers, screwdriver, wrench, hand drill, hammer, bits, small saw)

☐ Bailing wire

- [ ] Pipe clamps
- [ ] Extra screws, bolts, nuts, nails, washers to fit parts on frame
- [ ] Epoxy
- [ ] Replacement parts for any breakable item

First Aid Kit

- [ ] Triangular bandages
- [ ] Gauze rolls (two inches wide)
- [ ] Moleskin for blisters on hands or feet
- [ ] Assorted Band-Aids
- [ ] Sterile pads (four by four inches)
- [ ] Butterfly closures
- [ ] Safety pins
- [ ] First aid tape (two-inch size)
- [ ] Ace bandage
- [ ] Aspirin
- [ ] Antacid tablets
- [ ] Snake bite kit
- [ ] Tweezers
- [ ] First aid book
- [ ] Personal medications
- [ ] Drugs (if you decide to carry drugs, work with a medical doctor to learn correct dosages and possible side effects)

Clothing

- [ ] Wet suit (farmer John, wet suit jacket, wet suit bootees)

- [ ] Shoes to fit over wet suit bootees
- [ ] Hat and/or helmet
- [ ] Windbreaker or paddling jacket
- [ ] Wind pants or rain pants
- [ ] Rain gear (jacket and pants)
- [ ] Shorts and/or swimsuit
- [ ] T-shirt
- [ ] Wool or pile shirts or jackets or sweaters
- [ ] Wool pants
- [ ] Wool or synthetic long underwear
- [ ] Underwear
- [ ] Fiberfill or down jacket
- [ ] Wool stocking cap or balaclava
- [ ] Dry pair of shoes and clothing for in camp
- [ ] Leather gloves or Pogies

Personal Equipment

- [ ] Waterproof bag to carry personal clothing and equipment
- [ ] Life jacket
- [ ] Sleeping bag
- [ ] Sleeping pad
- [ ] Tarp or tent, with poles, stakes, etc.
- [ ] Flashlight, with spare batteries and bulb
- [ ] Candle for light in tent

- [ ] Personal items (toothbrush, toothpaste, hand lotion, glasses or contacts, towel or washcloth, biodegradable soap, razor, etc.)

- [ ] Eating utensils (cup, spoon, plate, etc.)

- [ ] Notebook and pen

- [ ] Knife, matches, fire starter (best if carried on your person)

- [ ] Insect repellent

- [ ] ChapStick

- [ ] Suntan lotion

- [ ] Sunglasses with safety strap

- [ ] Fishing gear and fishing license

- [ ] Camera, with film, lenses, etc.

Safety and Rescue Equipment

- [ ] Life jacket (one extra life jacket per raft may be required in some states or countries or by some agencies managing the river)

- [ ] Throw-rope rescue bags or ropes in each boat

- [ ] Signal mirror

- [ ] Winch with nonstretch rope

- [ ] Police whistle

Other Group Equipment

- [ ] Map with waterproof map case

- [ ] Compass

- [ ] Guidebook and other resource books about the river and area

- [ ] Water containers

- [ ] Purification tablets or other means of water purification

- [ ] Permit on rivers regulated by governmental agencies

- [ ] Matches and fire starter

- [ ] Ropes for lining boats

- [ ] Shovel

- [ ] Lantern

- [ ] Fire pan with grill

- [ ] Plastic garbage bags

- [ ] Burlap bags or nylon stuff bags to use over plastic garbage bags to prevent spills (also handy for carrying cooking pots, Dutch ovens, fire pan)

- [ ] Toilet paper

- [ ] Portable toilet or large ammo can, toilet seat, heavy-duty plastic bags, formaldehyde or lye (to be used to stop production of methane)

Cooking and Food Equipment

- [ ] Lightweight trips: pots, small stove and fuel, one cup and one spoon per person, food and spices

Luxurious-style trips:

- [ ] Dutch oven

- [ ] Frying pan

- [ ] Coffee pot

- [ ] Griddle

- [ ] Buckets

☐ Coolers and other food containers

☐ Spatula

☐ Large spoon

☐ Pliers

☐ Knives

☐ Can opener

☐ Burlap bags to hold Dutch ovens and pots

☐ Charcoal (when wood is scarce)

☐ Propane or gas stoves if fires are not used, with fuel

☐ Paper towels

☐ Dish soap and scrubber

☐ Clorox for sterilizing dishes and utensils

☐ Eating utensils for each person

☐ Food and spices

Kayaking

Choose clothing and equipment from the previous list that best meet your needs, plus the following:

☐ Kayak or decked canoe

☐ Paddle

☐ Flotation bags

☐ Small, waterproof, day storage bag to carry items that must be readily available

☐ Sponge

☐ Spray skirt

☐ Helmet

☐ Kayak repair kit (duct tape or fiber glass cloth, resin, catalyst)

☐ Spare break-down paddle

☐ Wet suit, with jacket, mittens or Pogies, hood, bootees

☐ Paddling jacket

☐ Throw-rope rescue bag

SOURCES OF INFORMATION AND EQUIPMENT

Information

Conservation.   In the United States, the main group working for protection of rivers is the:

> American Rivers Conservation Council
> 323 Pennsylvania Avenue, Southeast
> Washington, D.C. 20003

Periodicals

> *American Whitewater Journal*
> American Whitewater Affiliation
> Box 1483
> Hagerstown, Maryland 21740

> *Canoe*
> P.O. Box 10748
> Des Moines, Iowa 50349

> *Currents*
> National Organization for River Sports
> Box 6847
> Colorado Springs, Colorado 80934

Guidebooks.   The following sources can provide you with a list, including current prices and descriptions, of a wide variety of guidebooks and other river resource books:

Western United States

> Westwater Books
> Box 364
> Boulder City, Nevada 89005

United States

National Organization for River Sports
Resource Center
Box 6847
Colorado Springs, Colorado 80934

United States and Canada

American Canoe Association Book Service
P.O. Box 248
Lorton, Virginia 22079

England and Europe

British Canoe Union
Flexel House
45-47 High Street
Addlestone, Weybridge
Surrey KT15 IJV United Kingdom

Also see the "Periodicals" section.

Books. The following is an abbreviated list of the many books that are available on river running. Additional lists of books, as well as many of the books listed here, can be obtained from the groups listed under the "Guidebooks" section.

Advanced Fabrication Techniques for Whitewater Boats. Available from W. A. Clark and Associates, Sugarloaf Star Route, Boulder, Colorado 80302.

Arighi, Scott and Margaret. *Wildwater Touring.* New York: Macmillan Publishing Company, 1974.

Davidson, James, and Rugge, John. *The Complete Wilderness Paddler.* New York: Knopf, 1976.

Deschner, Whit. *Does the Wet Suit You?* Seattle: Eddie Tern Press, 1981.

Evans, Jay, and Anderson, Robert. *Kayaking.* Brattleboro, Vermont: The Stephen Greene Press, 1975.

Jenkinson, Michael. *Wild Rivers of North America.* New York: E. P. Dutton and Company, 1973.

Kinmont, Vikki, and Axcell, Claudia. *Simple Foods for the Pack.* San Francisco: Sierra Club Books, 1976.

Mason, Bill. *Path of the Paddle.* Toronto: Van Nostrand Reinhold, 1980.

McGinnis, William. *Whitewater Rafting.* New York: Times Books, 1975.

Mills, Sheila. *Rocky Mountain Kettle Cuisine.* Galley Impressions, 1980.

Norman, Dean, ed. *The All-Purpose Guide to Paddling.* Available from Great Lakes Living Press, 3634 West 216th Street, Matteson, Illinois 60443.

Steidle, Robert. *Wild-water Canoeing and Kayaking.* Paramus, New Jersey: Jolex, 1976.

Thomson, Barry, and Carothers, Steven. *The Enchanted Light: Images of the Grand Canyon* (photo essay). Flagstaff, Arizona: Museum of Northern Arizona Press, 1979.

Urban, John. *White Water Handbook.* 2d ed., rev. T. Walley Williams III. Appalachian Mountain Club, 1981.

Walbridge, Charles, and Rock, Steve. *Boatbuilder's Manual.* Penllyn, Pennsylvania: Wildwater Designs Kits, 1977.

Wilkerson, James. *Medicine for Mountaineering.* Seattle: The Mountaineers, 1967.

Regulated Rivers and Permit Information.   For rivers on public lands in the western United States, the *River Information Digest* by the Interagency Whitewater Committee is a good source, with information about regulations and permits. It is available sporadically from various Forest Service, Park Service, or Bureau of Land Management offices. If you have trouble getting one, send a self-addressed and stamped envelope to me:

c/o Outdoor Program
Box 8118
Idaho State University
Pocatello, Idaho 83209

River Maps

Western United States

Les Jones
Star Route, Box 13
Heber City, Utah 84032

Eastern United States

William Nealy's Maps
Nantahala Outdoor Center
Star Route, Box 68
Bryson City, North Carolina 28713

Water Levels.   For a list of the regional offices that have river flow information, write to the following national centers:

United States

Water Resources Division
United States Geological Survey
National Center
Reston, Virginia 22092

Office of Hydrology
National Weather Service
United States Department of Commerce
Silver Spring, Maryland 20910

Canada

Inland Waters Directorate
Water Resources Branch
Environment Canada
Ottawa, Ontario K1A 0E7

Topographic Maps

United States West of Mississippi

Branch of Distribution
United States Geological Survey
Federal Center
Denver, Colorado 80225

United States East of Mississippi

United States Geological Survey
1200 South Eads Street
Arlington, Virginia 22202

Canada

Map Distribution Office
615 Booth Street
Ottawa, Ontario K1A 0E9

Dominion Map Limited
541 Howe Street
Vancouver, British Columbia V6C 2C2

White-Water Schools.   Here are a few white-water schools that have good reputations. I do not mean by choosing these to belittle other fine schools that exist or new ones that are created each year. This list simply will give you a place to get started.

United States

Aspen Kayak School
P.O. Box 1520-C
Aspen, Colorado 81611

Nantahala Outdoor Center
Star Route, Box 68
Bryson City, North Carolina 28713
(Rafting and kayaking)

The Roger Paris Kayak School
Route 1, Box 9
Carbondale, Colorado 81623

Saco Bound/Northern Waters
Box 113
Center Conway, New Hampshire 03813
(Kayaking)

Sierra Kayak School
P.O. Box 682
Lotus, California 95651

Slickrock Kayaks
P.O. Box 1400
Moab, Utah 84532

Snake River Kayak School
P.O. Box 2098
Jackson, Wyoming 83001

Sundance Expeditions
14894 Galice Road
Merlin, Oregon 97532
(Rafting and kayaking)

Wolf River Lodge
White Lake, Wisconsin 54491
(Kayaking)

World of Whitewater
P.O. Box 708
Big Bar, California 96010
(Rafting and kayaking)

Canada

Capilano College
2055 Purcell Way
North Vancouver, British Columbia V7J 3H5
(Courses in white-water sports)

Madawaska Kanu Camp
2 Tuna Court
Don Mills, Ontario M3A 3L1

Outward Bound
P.O. Box 219
Keremeos, British Columbia V0X 1N0

Similkameen Wilderness Centre
Box 97
Cultus Lake, British Columbia V0X 1H0

Equipment

Selected companies from this list can provide you with any item described in this book. However, there also are many other fine companies that sell excellent products that are not included in this very abbreviated selection. I encourage you to check lists that appear in *Canoe* and *Currents* magazines (see the "Periodicals" section).

United States

Apple Line Company
R. D. 4
Washout Road
Scotia, New York 12302
(Kayaks)

B & A Distributing Company
2310 Northwest 24th Avenue
Portland, Oregon 97210
(Rafts and accessories)

Blackadar Boating
P.O. Box 1170
Salmon, Idaho 83467
(Kayaks, rafts, and accessories)

Camp-Ways
12915 South Spring Street
Los Angeles, California 92646
(Rafts and accessories)

Canham Whitewater Accessories
7815 Southeast Luther Road
Portland, Oregon 97206
(Rafts and accessories)

Cascade Outfitters
Route 1, Box 524
Monroe, Oregon 97456
(Kayaks, rafts, and accessories)

Class VI
3994 South 300 West, #8
Murray, Utah 84107
(Kayaks)

Dauber Canoe and Kayak
P.O. Box 59
Washington Crossing, Pennsylvania 18977
(Kayaks)

Dragon Fly Designs
P.O. Box 468
Geyserville, California 95441
(Accessories)

Easy Rider
P.O. Box 88108
Tukwila Branch C
Seattle, Washington 98188
(Kayaks)

Eddyline Northwest
8423 Mukilteo Speedway
Everett, Washington 98204
(Kayaks)

Extrasport
Suite 603, 3050 Biscayne Boulevard
Miami, Florida 33137
(Life vests and accessories)

Hollowform
6345 Variel Avenue
Woodland Hills, California 91364
(Kayaks)

Maravia Corporation
P.O. Box 395
San Leandro, California 94577
(Rafts)

Nantahala Outfitters
Star Route, Box 68
Bryson City, North Carolina 28713
(Kayaks and accessories)

Natural Designs
4849 West Marginal Way Southwest
Seattle, Washington 98106
(Kayaks)

Northwest River Supplies
P.O. Box 9186
Moscow, Idaho 83843
(Kayaks, rafts, and accessories)

Old Town Canoe Company
58 Middle Street
Old Town, Maine 04468
(Kayaks and accessories)

Perception
P.O. Box 686
Liberty, South Carolina 29657
(Kayaks)

Phoenix Products
U.S. Route 421
Tyner, Kentucky 40486
(Kayaks and accessories)

River Touring Equipment
341 Visitacion Avenue
Brisbane, California 94005
(Kayaks, rafts, and accessories)

Rogue Inflatables
P.O. Box 266
Grants Pass, Oregon 97526
(Rafts)

Salmon River Boatworks
P.O. Box 1804
Salmon, Idaho 83467
(Kayaks)

Seda Products
P.O. Box 997
Chula Vista, California 92012
(Kayaks and accessories)

Stearns Manufacturing Company
P.O. Box 1493
Saint Cloud, Minnesota 56301
(Life vests)

Voyageur's
P.O. Box 409
Gardner, Kansas 66030
(Accessories)

W. A. Clark and Associates
Sugarloaf Star Route
Boulder, Colorado 80302
(Kayak building supplies)

West Hills Outfitters
8425 Southwest 88th Avenue
Tigard, Oregon 97223
(Kayaks, rafts, and accessories)

Whitewater Boats
P.O. Box 483
Cedar City, Utah 84720
(Kayaks)

Wildwater Designs
230 Penllyn Pike
Penllyn, Pennsylvania 19422
(Accessories and kits)

Canada

Carleton Cycle and Outdoor Recreation
3201 Kingsway
Vancouver, British Columbia V5R 5K3
(Kayaks, canoes, and accessories)

Ecomarine Systems
1666 Duranleau Street
Granville Island
Vancouver, British Columbia V6H 3S4
(Kayaks, canoes, and accessories)

The Mountain Equipment Coop Limited
1820 Fir Street
Vancouver, British Columbia V6J 3B1
(Kayaks, canoes, and accessories)

The Mountain Equipment Coop Limited
131 12th Avenue Southeast
Calgary, Alberta T2G 0Z9
(Kayaks, canoes, and accessories)

INDEX

Boldface numerals indicate pages on which photographs, illustrations, or charts are located.

Other Books from Pacific Search Press

Messages from the Shore by Victor B. Scheffer

Minnie Rose Lovgreen's Recipe for Raising Chickens by Minnie Rose
    Lovgreen

Mushrooms 'n Bean Sprouts: A First Step for Would-be Vegetarians by
    Norma M. MacRae, R.D.

My Secret Cookbook by Paula Simmons

The Natural Fast Food Cookbook by Gail L. Worstman

The River Pioneers by Edwin Van Syckle

The Northwest Adventure Guide by Pacific Search Press

Rhubarb Renaissance: A Cookbook by Ann Saling

The Natural Fruit Cookbook by Gail L. Worstman

The Salmon Cookbook by Jerry Dennon

Seattle Photography by David Barnes

Sleek & Savage: North America's Weasel Family by Delphine Haley

Spinning and Weaving with Wool by Paula Simmons

Starchild & Holahan's Seafood Cookbook by Adam Starchild and James
    Holahan

They Tried to Cut It All by Edwin Van Syckle

Two Crows Came by Jonni Dolan

Warm & Tasty: The Wood Heat Stove Cookbook by Margaret Byrd Adams

The Whole Grain Bake Book by Gail L. Worstman

Wild Mushroom Recipes by Puget Sound Mycological Society

Wild Shrubs: Finding and Growing Your Own by Joy Spurr

The Zucchini Cookbook by Paula Simmons